WE THE WIDOWS

A GUIDE TO YOUR NEW LIFE

PATRICIA TYSON REDMOND

Epigraph

Death leaves a heart ache
No one can heal,
Love leaves a memory
No one can steal.

>   …From a headstone
>   in Ireland

"Say Their Name"

Someone I love has gone away
And life is not the same.
The greatest gift that you can give
Is just to speak their name.

I need to hear the stories
And the tales of days gone past.
I need for you to understand
Their memories must last.

We cannot make more memories,
Since they're no longer here.
So when you speak of them to me,
It's music to my ear.

>   …. Anonymous

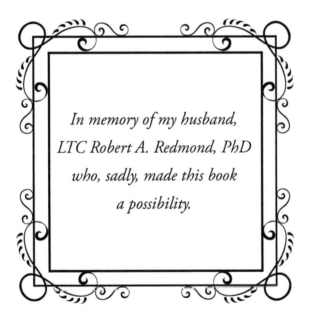

In memory of my husband,
LTC Robert A. Redmond, PhD
who, sadly, made this book
a possibility.

Table of Contents

1

Introduction to We the Widows

To all widows...welcome! This book is for you.

It is time to celebrate widows: you strong, confident women who have been getting along successfully in the world without the man you were married to for years...perhaps for many years. If you have successfully navigated widowhood without problems, congratulations. But undoubtedly there are many widows who aren't as confident and would like some help. The goal of this book is to offer that help: information, suggestions, some tips, some humor, and even some joy, to give you that support. After ten years of "practice" being a widow, and although still learning about this role, I hope to offer you some assistance by telling you about my journey.

This "widow" title is not exactly what a wife strives to achieve; it is just what happens when life does. We all have a plan for our lives, whether it is written in our journals or only in our minds. As you grow older, this generally includes plans for retirement, which will allow you and your husband the freedom to do...whatever. Many plans are made, dreams are dreamed, and you anticipate the day they can become a reality. However, that day may never come. The unthinkable happens; your husband falls off a ladder, is in an auto accident, develops an incurable cancer, or has a heart attack on the golf course. Now you are a widow! This was never in your plans, of course, but now it is your reality. What do you do now?

When my husband died making me a widow, I wasn't sure how I could survive. There were so many practical things in our lives that my husband took care of, leaving me no idea how to manage. I searched for information that would help me become a single person again after a 33-year marriage to my very best friend. I looked in the library for books written for and about widowhood but didn't find much help. So, I struggled on alone, missing my partner and soul mate and hoping that I could learn how to take care of myself again. Today, since the internet has permeated our culture, there is more information out there. However, since I decided back then that I would write a self-help guide for new widows, I am writing this now, ten years later, to share my findings with you. I have learned that memories are better than dreams, and we can do things we never thought possible. That includes a lot of things your husband might have told you were too difficult for you. I would like to share some of my widow life-lessons. Perhaps this will help you make an easier transition from wife to widow.

Yes, I have been thinking about writing this book for years, yet I have been procrastinating. I had lots of excuses not to write; I didn't have enough personal experiences, didn't know how to write a book, didn't have a good enough computer. But now, hopefully,

I do have these tools, and a daughter who said to me, when I told her I was going to write this book, "You said that last year!" So, no more stalling. Today is May 28, 2017, Memorial Day weekend, and I am at a campground in Virginia, just me and Rojo, my Irish Setter companion. I am secure in my little RV with a new laptop, lots of notes, and ready to go. I am committed; I am going to devote this summer to writing this book for you.

First, I will ask you if you feel you can't survive on your own and that there is nothing to live for, since you became a grieving widow. Grief doesn't come with directions that show you how to proceed. Everyone grieves differently and it takes time. I have learned that you take one day at a time believing that the sun will shine again. Until you feel like it will, trust God, and you will survive. This may sound like a cliché, but it's the truth. A newly widowed friend once told me, "I am vertical and ventilating… and still have a life to live!" And so do you!

Understandably, it is possible the independence and self-reliance that you had long ago, when you were single, young and energetic, has been submerged for many married years. These are years when you shared tasks with your husband, worked together and perhaps even leaned on him. With a little work and a lot of faith, you can again become that independent woman. Plus, now you have many years of life experiences and wisdom that you didn't have in your younger years. As you probably have determined by now, I am generally talking to the older widow, one who has been a part of a couple for years. Younger widows, especially if you have children to raise, are another story, and that book has already been written. (Widows Wear Stilettos: A Practical and Emotional

<u>Guide for the Young Widow,</u> by Carole Brody Fleet.) If you are a young widow you should have an easier time adapting to widowhood. However, there may be some information here that you can use, so don't stop reading.

Let me introduce myself, so we can become friends...sisters in the same society. I am a Christian, a mother, a grandmother, a retired physical therapist who never worked a day in her life, (but more about that later), a member of the Daughters of the American Revolution, and a Red Hatter. I love to read, to travel, to take photos, to camp and to kayak. I am a sponsor of Wreaths Across America; I record veterans' stories for the Veterans History Project in partnership with the Library of Congress. I am also now "half a couple" ...a widow.

I have learned to enjoy life fully, one must have some passion in life. Find something that you love to do, something that makes you happy and gives you satisfaction. Something you can wake up looking forward to. Perhaps it is something that was on your "bucket list" or something new that you think you'd like to do or learn. It could be volunteer work, tutoring, traveling, creating pottery or sewing. The list is endless. Choose something you will look forward to and something that will keep you occupied.

Know that you will make mistakes. Just laugh at yourself, forgive yourself and get on with it. You will have big decisions to make, like buying a new car, a major appliance, hot water tank, or selling your home. Think of it as another adventure. Problems will undoubtedly occur. Things happened when you were a couple and they will still happen, but you will learn how to deal with them. We can't control what happens, but we can control our reaction to the event. Six months after my husband died, when we had a major storm, a huge tree fell, knocking a lot of surrounding tree branches down with it. I cried when I saw what a mess my back yard was and was disappointed to find that I wouldn't have firewood for the next few years from this 90-foot poplar tree that had to be hauled away at a great expense. Nevertheless, I got it done and was stronger for successfully dealing with it.

Be brave and take an honest look at your own life and acknowledge the changes that need to be made. It takes courage to act on these changes. Take your time and consider all the angles. For example, it is advisable to stay in the home you have been living in for at least a year after you become a widow. If you make an earlier move, you may regret it later. To quote one of my widow friends, "My advice is to be really thoughtful and to make no quick decisions. I can attest to the folly of this. I too hastily put a down payment on an apartment at a local retirement community, where I had many friends. I put my home on the market, had a potential sale for it, and found myself in tears when planning to leave it. So…I undid it all, took my home off the market, got my deposit back and have been happily living in my nine-room three-bath 1903 Victorian home for the past seven years."

I am still living in our same home and am only thinking of moving into a retirement home in the future. I am glad that I stayed where the memories are. However, you may come to a different decision. Another widow couldn't wait to move out of the home they had shared together after her husband of 33 years deteriorated and died there of Alzheimer's disease. Her home was full of sad memories. Determine what is important to you and what you want to do. Then set goals and a plan for achieving these goals.

As I said above, we all make wrong choices, struggle over problems or do things we regret. But to quote a life-changing speaker and author, Dr. Steve Maraboli, "You are not your mistakes; you are not your struggles. You are here and now with the power to shape your day and your future." Therefore, don't blame yourself when you make a mistake; just forgive yourself, learn from the mistake, and move on. Your happiness is in your hands. It is your job to be happy and no one else's. I have found that if you have a positive attitude, put on a smile and act happy, you may be surprised to discover that you are happy. Learn to laugh at yourself. That is, don't take yourself too seriously. I have decided that if I become egocentric now people won't notice if I become senile.

However, before...and if...that occurs, there is another widow's suggestions to report. She writes, "Keep up with the happenings in our world, our country and your community. Do read as many newspapers, magazines, and books as you can. Don't apologize for watching TV; there is much to be learned from it when you are selective. By all means, allow your neighbors to come into your life. I have had two new young neighbors with small children recently and they are delightful and so kind to this 96-year-old." This will keep you interesting and prevent you from becoming a "bore" ...perhaps.

You may already have adult children and are a grandmother. Congratulations! Grandchildren are wonderful. However, now that granddad is no longer here, you may find it difficult to continue the traditions that had been established over the years. I have found that it is much easier to go to the children and their family homes than to get them to come to mine. As I remarked one Thanksgiving, when my grandchildren were saying what they were most thankful for, "I am glad that I like to drive better than I like to cook!" This is really true...I haven't really liked to cook for years, and a widow doesn't have to cook three meals a day to feed a hungry husband. (See, there are benefits to being a widow!) Conversely, you may like to cook and your family may still continue to come home for the holidays. However, if they don't you will have to adapt and accept their decisions...and without complaints. The lessons here are; love your children but don't rely on them to take over for your husband or become the center of your life. They have their own lives to live. Furthermore, don't make them feel guilty for anything they don't do for you. If they don't call you, call them. Center you call around them, not you or your problems. Don't criticize your sons-in-law...daughters have enough problems with them. Become your own person. Realize that this is just one of the many changes in your life. And don't forget...they may be the ones who pick out your nursing home when you are unable, so be nice!

The pitty-patter of the rain on my roof makes me feel warm, comfortable and protected. It brings back memories of our many camping experiences. Enjoying it is something that I can do by myself; I can still enjoy God's awesome nature all by myself! But I digress; back to the book. I am not going to proselytize, but I do believe that one needs the help of our Creator to get through difficult times in life. However, even if you don't believe, I hope and pray that my words will still be of help to you. I've been told by several divorced women that being divorced is in many ways quite similar to being a widow. That is, the person feels the absence of the husband who was a helpmate. So perhaps I will have a wider audience for this book. Whatever, come along with me and learn ways to solve problems, consider new ideas, and explore new ways to look at your life.

I do want to clarify something, so you don't get the wrong impression. I am not a psychologist; I don't have a master's degree in counseling, an MBA, or a medical degree, and I am not related to Heloise. I'm just a widow who had a lot of questions when I became a single person again. I am writing this because I am a widow with a desire to help other widows and I like to write. Some of my suggestions and tips may help you. I would like to entertain you as well as enlighten you about a number of things. I hope you will enjoy reading this book about widowhood.

In the past ten years, I have talked to many widows and will include their comments, ideas and suggestions, what has helped them the most and what didn't work for them. A concern most mentioned was the loneliness of being a widow, of living alone, building a life without your husband, and accepting his absence. Many said that you should keep busy. "Have a plan for each day and don't isolate yourself. Find new interests, accept invitations, and establish your own routine." For so many of us, going to church will be a renewal time. Faith is a big part of this. One widow wrote, "God is my best friend. He has created an entire new life for me and I will try to do my best with Him at my side forever."

Yes, we the widows have a different life than we had thought and hoped for, but remember that it's your life, your own life now, and you can get control. It will take work, a lot of prayers...and a belief in yourself to make it the best life. So, let's get started.

Yesterday is history; tomorrow a mystery; today is a gift...that is why it's called the present! Go forth and become your new confident self.

2

New Widow Basics

It may be a bit presumptuous of me to even write the following: Many you have no doubt already done these things. Perhaps you had discussed issues with your husband and made many decisions together, so now you can just carry out his final wishes. On the other hand, if your husbands' death was caused by an accident you may not have been prepared, so I will try to give some ideas of what to expect.

One of the largest challenges a widow faces is a failure of communication between them, prior to her husband's death. Questions about locations of the important paperwork, security codes, pin numbers and addresses, especially in this internet age, funeral decisions, how to resolve ownership of property...these are the questions that should be answered prior to death. You may not know all the information below, but if you know where the paperwork is stored, you should be able to find what out is needed and this will make decisions easier.

This is where you start if you are a recent widow. There are a lot of practical matters and issues you will need to take care of as soon as possible. The list of what you will need is below and then on following pages I will elaborate on each one. The information listed may have changed since this guide was written in 2017. I'm including is a list of resources, with phone numbers and websites, so that you can research and verily the information.

You will undoubtedly need the following items:

IDENTIFICATION

- Husband's driver's license
- His Social Security card or number
- DD-214 form or any paperwork pertaining to military service
- Passport

OFFICIAL DOCUMENTS

- Death Certificates.
- Husband's will
- Marriage certificate
- Mortgage papers
- Citizenship Documents
- Life insurance policies, any other insurance policies, such as funeral, long-term care, home insurance, Survivor Benefit Plan (SBP)
- Automobile titles, RV, boat or any vehicle titles

FINANCIAL

- Checkbooks
- Savings accounts
- Any financial accounts; CD's, IRA's, 401K's
- Credit cards
- Loans
- Separate accounts or accounts held jointly

OTHER IMPORTANT ITEMS

- Household utilities information (telephone, gas, electric, internet, etc.)
- Husband's cell phone
- Memberships, magazine subscription information
- Digital accounts, such as email, Facebook or other social media

It will help if you keep a journal or notebook so information won't be lost or misplaced. Do allow others to help you with this. Be in charge, but delegate. Many items on the list can be done for you by someone else.

Tips: Don't throw any paperwork away initially. You may need it later.

Don't panic! Things will be taken care of. Everything doesn't have to be done immediately, and you can get help with those that do.

Funeral and Memorial Services

Along with dealing with all of the above, you will immediately have a funeral home to select, a funeral or memorial service to plan, and a casket to pick out. Your funeral director can help you decide the type of disposition (the final handling of the deceased's remains), whether an earth burial, above ground burial, or cremation. If you are not a member or attend a local church, the funeral director can recommend a minister or official to perform the funeral or memorial service, and you will need to decide on a location for the burial. You will choose family or friends you would like to give a eulogy, choose the pallbearers, (traditionally there are six) the readings and the music for the service. The funeral staff or your church can create a program for the funeral or memorial service. A guest book allows you to know who attended the visitation and funeral, and you may purchase one from the funeral home or from a stationery store.

Perhaps you will want to write an obituary to put in your local papers to for notify friends and associates. (Most newspapers charge for obituaries.) Generally, the funeral home will submit your obituary for you. You will decide if you want a viewing for a day or two prior to the funeral, and if you want flowers on the casket. You will pick out clothing for your husband to wear in the casket and decide if you will have an open or closed one during the viewing. (Some widows prefer to have only family present for the service.) You will have to decide where he is to be buried, either in your local cemetery or elsewhere, and you will have to purchase a cemetery plot. Later, you can decide on a headstone for the burial plot.

Note: Once you have selected the funeral home the staff will undoubtedly help you with a lot of the necessary tasks and paperwork. An unexpected extra: I supplied photos of my husband and they put together a marvelous slide show of his life that ran in a loop during the visitation hours.

CREMATION

Choosing cremation in no way interferes with having a "traditional funeral." However, if your husband is to be cremated, you will still have a lot of decisions to make. Will you have a viewing and a funeral with the body in a casket? Some funeral homes offer cremation caskets for temporary use during visitation prior to cremation. If not, you will have to purchase a casket and that will be an expense, but the body can be cremated in the casket. (Funeral homes require some sort of container to hold the body for the cremation.) The cremains (ashes) will require a container (urn) as well, which can be either buried in a cemetery, placed in a niche in a columbarium or you can keep them and/or scatter them as you wish. If you do select entombment in a mausoleum or columbarium, you will need to purchase a crypt specifically designed for that purpose. With both interment (burial below ground) and inurnment (above ground in a niche wall or columbarium) you may need to purchase a burial vault or grave liner depending on the cemetery's rules.

Another unconventional option is to use the cremains to create an artificial coral reef which serves as a marine habitat, helps prevent erosion and serves as a permeant living legacy. The cremation ashes are mixed with environmentally safe concrete and molded into a hollow structure that's up to 6-foot-wide and 5-foot-tall that sits on the sea floor. For more information on this, you can Google Eternal Reefs, the Reef Ball Foundation or just ask the funeral director.

If you chose cremation, you may be interested in cremation jewelry. Some of the ashes can be enclosed in a pendant so you can keep your loved one close to your heart. I do have two friends who have done this. One widow has a dime-sized silver disc with her husband's fingerprint on one side. The other widow has a gold heart with an inscription. Both ladies wear these necklaces continuously, and it gives them comfort. You can Google "cremation jewerly" or ask your funeral director for information about this type of keepsake.

I would be remiss if I omitted telling you about having the ashes made into a diamond. Ashes are carbon and under extreme pressure and high heat, they become a diamond. It is the same process that is used for making artificial diamonds. Sounds like it could be the final revenge of a widow who never got that "promised diamond" her husband talked about for years. However, the process is expensive, but if you want more information, you can look up "ashes to diamonds" or go to the website info@lifegem.com .

HEADSTONE OR MARKER

Once you have chosen a cemetery the staff there will work with your funeral director to have your chosen plot prepared for the funeral and burial. However, the headstone doesn't have to be decided on immediately. Later, the cemetery officials will help you decide on a grave marker or headstone.

ANATOMICAL GIFTS

Donating organs or tissues for transplant may be a significant way to help others. Your physician or a local organ donation agency can provide more information about anatomical gifts. This is a time sensitive issue but the transplant procedures don't interfere with preparing a body for a funeral service. Information about organ and tissue donation and transplantation is available at www. organdonor.gov or the United Network for Organ Sharing at www.unos.org.

This is a decision that can be made by a family just prior to the death of a loved one, if it has not previously been decided. Anyone with a driver's license can make this decision. The DMV will put a small heart on your driver's license to indicates that you have chosen to be an organ donor at death. It's comforting to know that you have the power to donate life!

EXPENSES INVOLVED

In the United States the average cost for a funeral runs from $7,000 to $10,000. Some will cost more, but generally not less. There are really three main components involved: what is paid for the services of the funeral home, director and staff, what is paid for the services of the cemetery, and what is paid for the headstone or grave marker. A cremation will cost less, of course, but still the average price is between $2,500 and $3,500 for all the expenses involved. Keep in mind that the prices may vary greatly, depending on different funeral homes and their location in the country.

Note: Please be Aware! Unfortunately, not all who read the obituaries are friends and family. It is advisable to have someone stay in your home during the time of the funeral, "just in case" thieves consider it an opportune time to break into your home. In addition, you could be contacted via phone, mail or email by someone dealing in funeral or cemetery merchandise. These contacts may or may not be from unscrupulous persons. If you do receive a call and have concerns, you can contact your funeral home for information.

INFORMATION FOR THE MILITARY CONNECTED

If your husband was a veteran or active duty military, the following is information you will find helpful.

DEATH OF A RETIRED SOLDIER

If your husband was in the Army, your can contact the Department of the Army Casualty and Mortuary Affairs Operations Center anytime by calling 800-626-3317. You will be referred to a local Casualty Assistance Center who will report the death to the Defense Finance and Accounting Service (DFAS: 800-321-1080 www.dfas.mil) to stop retired pay and initiate the survivor benefits process. If you live close to a military installation and would like assistance with military administrative matters, this can be arranged. When reporting the death, please provide as much of the information below as you have: (This information is valid for all services.)

- Full name
- Marital status
- Next of kin
- Social Security number and service number
- Circumstances surrounding the death
- Retirement date
- Copy of the death certificate
- Retired rank
- Copy of the Statement of Service (last DD214 form)

OTHER MILITARY ASSOCIATIONS

For the survivor of a military spouse, there are additional considerations. Some associations offer spouse assistance to their members, including the following:

- Military Officers Association of America: 800-234-6622 www.moaa.org
- Army and Air Force Mutual Aid Association: 800-336-4538 or 703-552-3060 www.aafmaa.com
- Navy Mutual Aid Association: 800-628-6011 or 703-614-1638 www.navymutal.org
- Department of Veterans Affairs or Veterans Administration (VA): www.va.gov or call 1-800-827-1000. (You will have to listen to the prompts very carefully to get to the person who has info you want.)

ADDITIONAL CONTACTS WHICH MAY BE HELPFUL

Arlington National Cemetery for funeral service: 877-907-8585 www.arlingtoncemetery.mil/funerals

Army Emergency Relief Services:866-878-6378 www.arehq.org

Defense Enrollment Eligibility Reporting System, for ID cards and benefits, 800-538-9552 www.dmdc.osd.mil

Navy-Marine Corps Relief Society, 800-654-8364 www.nmcrs.org

TRICARE: East: 800-444-5445 West: 877-874-2273 www.tricare.mil

DD-214 FORM

This is a document of the US Department of Defense, issued upon a military service member's retirement, separation, or discharge from active duty in the Armed Forces of the United States. It is essential to establish eligibility in a national cemetery. To locate a missing copy of the DD-214 contact the US National Archives and Records Administration at 1-866-272-6274 www.archives.gov

SURVIVOR BENEFIT PLAN

The Survivor Benefit Plan (SBP) is an elective insurance plan that will pay the surviving spouse a monthly payment (annuity) to help make up for the loss of her husband's retirement income. Not every veteran chooses this plan upon his retirement. There are monthly payments taken out of his retirement income (approximately 6.5% of his gross pay/month) that start immediately after his date of retirement until his demise.

Unfortunately, there is a SBP/DIC offset for the 57,000 surviving military spouses which includes me. It is a situation in which surviving spouses who become eligible for Dependency and Indemnity Compensation (DIC) from the VA, but are also covered by the SBP, have their SBP benefit reduced by the amount of DIC benefits received. For most survivors, multiple annuities can be paid upon the service members death. For military spouses… and military spouses only…the government requires that SBP be deducted from the DIC annuities. So those payments that my husband made every month for 20 years are cut drastically. This SBP/DIC offset is called the "widows tax", by the way. Congress can "fix" it and we widows can receive the full amount…but they have failed to do so.

Note: You must notify the DFAS immediately after your husband's death. They will send a form to complete and return (DD2656-7). When DFAS receives this form, they will begin the SBP annuity your husband paid for, thinking it would help you live a comfortable life after his death.

BURIAL IN A NATIONAL CEMETERY

Any retired veteran who was honorably discharged and who was qualified for retired pay is entitled to a free burial in a national cemetery. This eligibility also extends to some civilians who have provided military-related service and some Public Health Service personnel. Spouses and dependent children also are entitled to a plot and marker when buried in a national cemetery. While there is not a VA national cemetery in every state, there are 135 national cemeteries in the United States, including Puerto Rico. The Department of the Army National Cemetery maintains two national cemeteries, Arlington National Cemetery in Arlington, VA and the US Soldiers and Airmen's Home National Cemetery in Washington, DC. There are no charges for opening or closing the grave, for a vault or liner, or for setting the government headstone or marker in a national cemetery. The family generally is responsible for other expenses including transportation to the cemetery. Contact your state Veterans Affairs Office or visit the Department of Veterans Affairs' website. To reach the regional veterans office in your area, call 1-800-827-1000. Website: www.va.gov or call the National Cemetery Administration at 866-900-6417 Website: www.cem.va.gov

If your husband had not decided where he would prefer to be buried, you must decide if he will be buried at a military cemetery, such as Arlington National Cemetery (ANC). Eligibility requirements for interment are different from other national cemeteries. Eligibility for in-ground burial at Arlington National Cemetery is the most stringent of all US national cemeteries. However, most veterans, who have at least one day of active service for other than training and an honorable discharge are eligible for above ground inurnment in the columbarium.

If you do choose burial at a national cemetery and your husband qualifies, you will probably want to have a local funeral or memorial service soon after his death, because the interment (or inurnment) at least at Arlington National Cemetery, won't be scheduled for three to six months due to the number of funerals scheduled daily. Your funeral director will contact the cemetery and get a date set for the interment. On this date, you may decide to have a short ceremony in the Fort Myers Chapel prior to the service at the gravesite. However, although this is nice, it is not necessary and you may not be able to schedule the Chapel.

Funeral attendees can meet at the Administration Building on the grounds and drive together to the burial area. The entire procedure will be well organized by the ANC staff. You may want to plan a luncheon or dinner for the attendees after the interment and if so, can use the Fort Myers Officers Club which is now open to all ranks or make other arrangements.

BURIAL IN A STATE VETERANS CEMETERY

Many states have established veterans cemeteries and offer burial options for veterans and their families. These cemeteries have similar eligibility requirements but some other details many vary. Usually residence in the state is required. Even though they may have been established with government funds through the VA's Veterans Cemetery Grants Program, state veterans cemeteries are run solely by the states. To locate one of the state veterans cemeteries, visit www.cem.va.com or Google state veterans cemetery.

HEADSTONE OR MARKER

If your husband is buried in a military cemetery, you will decide what will be engraved on the headstone. You will not have to purchase one; it will be provided by the military cemetery. You are allowed a maximum of eleven lines engraved on the marker. (This is the case if buried at Arlington National Cemetery, you will need to find out the procedures at other military cemeteries.) If you are unsure what to include on the marker, you can ask one of his military friends or the cemetery staff for assistance. I had some difficulty convincing the staff that my husband's medals be written out instead of just the initials and to include PhD on the headstone.

Many of the above plans can be already in place if you and your husband are prepared for his death. My husband picked out the funeral home and casket he would like and decided to be buried at Arlington instead of West Point. This made decisions a lot easier for me at the end.

NAVY MUTUAL AID ASSOCIATION INFORMATION

Note: For further information, I have permission to include a copy of the Navy Mutual Survivor Checklist and the Navy Mutual Planning Checklist. (Appendices Section before References). They are more specific to the requirements of one who was in the military, regardless of the service. The Navy Mutual Planning Checklist will be useful for you to complete, so your family will be prepared after your death.

If you want to contact Navy Mutual for additional information, their number is: 800-628-6011 www.navymutual.org

MORE IMPORTANT MATTERS TO BE CONSIDERED

The funeral is over. Now you can take a breath and know that you are through with a big part of saying good bye to your loved one. However, there are a lot of things you will do now to make sure all your personal business affairs legal and secure. The below will identify procedures and task necessary to do so. You won't have to do this alone, you can get help from your family, your lawyer, professional advisor, or anyone else you choose. Just be careful that you deal with professional people who are well identified to you. (I will talk about scams and other possible problems in later chapters.)

POWER OF ATTORNEY

A Power of Attorney (POA) is a document that allows you to appoint a person or organization to manage your affairs if you become unable to do so. All POA's are not created equal. Each type gives you a different level of control.

Couples should have in place a durable financial power of attorney. This makes it easier for the spouse to handle the finances if the other becomes incapacitated. While medical or financial POA's can't prevent accidents, or keep you young, they can make life easier for you and your family if things do happen. However, this will automatically expire when the spouse dies.

DEATH CERTIFICATES

A death certificate is an official government-issued document that declares the date and time, location and cause of death as well as other personal information about the person who died. Legally a death certificate must be issued when death occurs. It will be necessary as you make funeral arrangements and take care of the deceased person's business. The death must be registered with the local or state vital records office within a matter of days, generally five or less. The death certificate must be signed by a medical professional: either the primary physician, attending physician, non-attending physician, medical examiner, nurse practioner, forensic pathologist, or coroner. This varies according to state law.

There are several ways to obtain a death certificate. The funeral home you are working with can get certified copies, you can order certified copies from a third-party company, or you can order copies yourself from the Vital Records Office at your local Health Department or the Division of Vital Records in the state in which the person died.

Note: The funeral home may charge you more for the certificates if they do obtain them. You can decide if it's worth the bother to get them yourself. However, it will be more expedient to obtain them through the funeral home or at least from your local Vital Records Office. If you order death certificates from the Division of Vital Records, it will take three to four weeks.

In my case, the funeral home contacted my husband's primary care physician to complete the death certificate, which they would file with the Vital Records Office at the local Health Department. When I received the death certificate, I felt that the physician listed an incorrect official cause of death on the certificate. There were also some other spelling mistakes which were minor, but still important on the official certificate. For some reason, I could not discuss the apparent mistakes with the doctor directly. I provided sufficient information to the funeral home and they passed it on to my husband's physician, who then agreed to list cancer caused by exposure to Agent Orange when in Vietnam had contributed to the cause of his death. A second amended death certificate was provided. My point is that you should carefully read the death certificate and make sure all the facts listed are correct. It is an official, government document and should be amended if there are mistakes.

The funeral home advised me to get twenty death certificates. I followed their advice and ended up with twelve unused ones. Not every organization requires an original death certificate, sometimes a copy will suffice. You should inquire which is required before sending an original. The cost for an official death certificate varies from state to state but is generally between $10.00 to $20.00.

Perhaps you will discover later that you want more official copies of the death certificate. Again, you can go to your local Department of Vital Records or contact the Division of Vital Records in your state. States have different regulations, and you must contact the home state of the deceased. You can research the information on the internet. Just ask how to get a death certificate in whatever state you are interested in. Once you determine the cost per copy, and the number of copies you need, you can send a check or money order.

For example, in the state of Maryland, you would write to:

Division of Vital Records
PO Box 68760
Baltimore, MD 21215-0036

You will need to include your name, address, phone number, email address, relationship to the deceased, photocopy of a current government issued ID, name of the deceased, date of death, age at death, sex, place of death, name of funeral home, reason for requesting certificate and a self-addressed, stamped envelope.

Note: The Division of Vital Records will never ask for your Social Security Number or Credit Card PIN when processing requests for copies of vital records.

There is an organization called Everplans that has a lot of useful information online. (Google: Everplans Funeral) I am not endorsing this company since I have not dealt with them, just describing who they are and what they do. This is a quote from their website: "Everplans is a complete archive of everything your loved ones will need should something happen to you. Securely store wills, passwords, funeral wishes, and more in your own secure and shareable vault." Actually, this sounds like a useful plan to have in place. I have always been concerned about "lost passwords" and I do tend to lose mine at times, even now. I was fortunate that my husband always used the same password for everything and I knew what it was. This was over ten years ago when cybercrime wasn't such an issue and we weren't concerned about being hacked. Everplans website has a lot of information about planning a funeral and end-of-life resources which is free. However, there is a fee if you register for their services.

A similar service is provided for active duty military, veterans and their wives who are members of the Army and Air Force Mutual Aid Association. Telephone: 800-336-4538 or 703-522-3060. This is a free service. I can personally vouch for it; my will and information are stored there. It is secure.

WILL

A will is a written document that directs the disposition of your property; it is wise to have a will in place for a number of reasons.

The most important is generally a will resolves a lot of the questions you might have upon your husband's death. A will does not affect the disposition of property that is titled in both of your names as "joint owners with the right of survivorship". Property with both your names will automatically belong to you, the surviving joint owner, regardless of the deceased's will.

If your husband had a will, you will probably know who his lawyer was or can find this information in the paperwork. You can contact the lawyer to check if the will must be probated. Probate is a legal process that takes place after someone dies. It involves the Department of Vital Records at your local county court house and perhaps a lawyer. However, since states have different laws, you may not need to probate his will. Most states allow a certain amount of property to pass free of probate or through a simple probate procedure. Also, property that passes outside of your will, through joint tenancy or a living trust does not need to be probated.

If your husband did not have a will…. this is called intestate… the state where you live will decide what to do with his estate. For example, if you live in Virginia and your husband died without a will, the courts will divide your husband's estate equally among you and your children. If you have three children, you and each child will inherit a quarter of the estate. His stepchildren, if not adopted, will not be included in this settlement. Since states laws vary, your state may divide the estate differently.

Yes, states have different rules and regulations regarding wills. The Maryland State Bar Association has a very informative free brochure entitled "Wills and Estates". I imagine most states bar associations will offer similar information.

SOCIAL SECURITY SURVIVORSHIP

As a widow, you may be eligible for a share of your husband's Social Security allotment. In the United States, a widow can receive Social Security benefits following the death of her husband even though she may not have made contributions to the Social Security System in her lifetime. The survivor's Social Security benefit is determined by a complex set of rules. You can notify Social Security by calling the national toll-free service at 1-800-772-1213 (TTY 1-800-325-0778*) or visiting your local Social Security office. An appointment is not required, but if you call ahead and schedule one, it may reduce the time you spend waiting to apply. They will provide information on what action needs to be taken.

You may need to provide documents such as:

> proof of death, birth certificate or other proof of birth, proof of U.S. citizenship, U.S. military discharge papers, W-2 forms and/or self-employment tax returns for last year, marriage certificate.

They accept photocopies of W-2 forms, self-employment tax returns or medical documents, but must see the original of most other documents, such as birth certificate. These will be returned to you. Also bring your checkbook or other papers that show your account number at a bank, credit union or other financial institution so you can sign up for Direct Deposit. They will ask your name and Social Security number; your maiden name, your husband's date and place of birth, Social Security number, date of death and place of death. They will also ask your citizenship status, whether you have used any other Social Security number, if he was in the military, and possibly other questions. If you don't have all the answers, they will assist you in getting them.

Social Security provides a one-time death benefit of $255 to surviving spouses, if you meet certain requirements. (Spouse must be married for nine months or more and living in the same household as the deceased, who must have been "insured" or had at least 40 quarters of employment.) Obviously, this amount does not come close to covering the expenses involved with a funeral. However, you are allowed to keep the last Social Security check your spouse receives, even if it is received during the month in which he died. (Social Security checks are paid retroactively. For example, if your spouse died on May 7, he had lived the whole month of April and you can keep the check which was received by May 7.) However, this is a bit complicated, so it is best to check with the local Social Security office.

*(TTY is a device that lets people who are deaf, hard of hearing, or speech impaired use the telephone to communicate by allowing them to type messages back and forth to one another instead of talking. TTY stands for teleprinter or teletypewriter. A TTY is required at both ends of the conversation in order to communicate.)

FINANCIAL INVESTMENTS, BANKS, AND SECURITIES

You need to inform all accounts of his death. Some will require an original death certificate, others will accept a copy. If you have joint investment accounts or investment accounts held in your husband's name these will need to be addressed. Investments include IRA's, stocks and bonds, mutual funds, 401k's, pension funds, military benefits, 529 college savings, just to name a few.

CREDIT CARDS

Make a complete list of your spouse's credit cards, debit cards, phone cards, business expense accounts, and any other open account he may have had. Each of these institutions needs to be notified of his death, and many will require a copy of the death certificate to validate your request to close the account. Ask each company whether there is any applicable insurance that pays off the account in the event of death. Check auto loans, credit cards and mortgages for this type of insurance. In addition, notify all three credit reporting agencies and request a current copy of the deceased's credit report.

Note: The three credit reporting agencies are Equifax, Experian, and TransUnion.

LIFE INSURANCE POLICIES

If your husband had life insurances policies, it is advisable to contact the companies immediately. You will find the contact information on the policy. The insurance money will be useful to help you pay the funeral expenses. If your husband was still working, you can also check with your husband's employment, to see if the company has addition insurance in place or any spousal benefits or entitlements, and if you are employed, check with your company to see if you have bereavement leave benefits available.

MARRIAGE CERTIFICATE

You will need an original copy of your marriage certificate for many reasons; for Social Security, insurance, etc. If you can't find the original, you can get a certified copy from the Division of Vital Records. You can Google the information: (name your state) Department of Vital Records. That appears to work. Also, the National Center for Health Statistics can help. Their website lists each state and contact information for vital records. Their website is: www.edc/nchs/howto/w2/w2welcome.htm (Highlight "Where to Write for Vital Records-Homepage" and then select your state.)

MORTGAGE PAPERS

If your name is listed jointly on the mortgage, you will need to inform the mortgage company and become the sole owner of your residence. You will also need to know when the monthly mortgage is due and how it is paid.

AUTOMOBILE TITLES

Contact the Department of Motor Vehicles (DMV) for information on updating the registration and title of the automobiles. Generally, you need not change the titles immediately, but will need a copy of the death certificate if you do. You will need it also to sell the vehicle.

Check your automobile insurance to see if you need to discontinue auto insurance on your husbands' vehicle. You will need to keep the insurance until you dispose of the car and turn in the plates to the DMV.

HOUSEHOLD UTILITIES

Check all your utility bills to see if your name is also on the account. Most companies require you have your name on the account to act as administrator. Some accounts will have to be closed and reopened in your name on the account. This is especially true for internet companies. I had to take my husband's death certificate to my internet service to prove he was dead before they would put my name on the account or allow me to make any changes in our contract with them. In addition, the contract has to expire or one pays an exorbitant rate to cancel, unless family can prove the one whose name is on the contract has died.

CELL PHONE

Locate your husband's cell phone. You may want to preserve his voicemail message in another form, as it may be deleted accidentally if the phone malfunctions or the service contract is ended. Contracts can generally be canceled with a death certificate. However, I would suggest that if your husband's voice is on your answering machine, it be changed after his death. Some caller may not know he is dead and all that entails, and even those who do know could get a surprise to hear his voice.

MAGAZINES, PERIODICALS, MEMBERSHIP FEES

You might want to cancel the subscriptions of magazines or memberships that only your husband held. Some magazine subscriptions renew automatically unless cancelled.

OTHER CANCELLATIONS

Sort through official paperwork to look for personal accounts, outstanding appointments, upcoming trips that may need to be cancelled, or anything that must be dealt with before a cancellation charge applies.

EMERGENCY CONTACTS

You may need to change emergency contacts. This is especially important if there are minor children in the family.

CITIZENSHIP DOCUMENTATION

You may need proof of American citizenship, such as a passport or voting registration card.

DRIVER'S LICENSE

Your husband's driver's license may be necessary for identification. However, you should contact the DMV to cancel it and so they will have a record of his death.

ADDITIONAL CONSIDERATIONS

You will also have the distribution of your husband's clothes and personal items to consider. This doesn't have to be done immediately and you can take your time. Perhaps you will want to let family members and friends have something as a memento to remember him by. Clothes can always be donated to a charity or given to family members. It is an onerous task when you are dealing with his loss and you may have to force yourself to take it on. Hopefully your family or a close friend can help out. There is a positive to this; look at all the closet space you will have after you have finished.

Note: I made "Memory Bears" from his neckties for each of my husband's siblings and our children. Serendipitously, I found a box of his military medals on the top shelf of his closet which I used to decorate the bears. This was well appreciated and will be a reminder of him in the future. If you are a seamstress, you can just Google "How to Make Memory Bears" or check on Pinterest for a pattern and free tutorial.

THOSE PRECIOUS WEDDING RINGS

One question a lot of widows have asked is when do you take off your wedding rings? There is no definitive answer to this question; it is just how you personally feel. You can continue to wear them for the rest of your life if you so please. There may be a day that you feel you can take them off. It doesn't change anything. You were married and now you aren't; you are a widow. Some widows decide to wear their engagement ring on the right hand and that is a perfectly good idea, especially if you are really attached to it. Sometimes I still will wear my engagement ring which was a miniature of my husband's West Point graduation ring. Other widows take their rings off after they become loose on their finger and they fear they may lose them.

Personally, I wore my wedding rings for the first year I was widowed. Prior to that, I had my husband's gold wedding band formed into a heart that I wore on a chain around my neck. When I took off my wedding rings, I also had a heart made out of my gold wedding band and put it on the same chain. It is a lot smaller and fits inside my husband's "heart". I have worn this necklace for ten years now, and it gives me comfort in times of stress or loneliness. I remember that I was loved and that gives me the strength to deal with the problem or make the decision. In Chapter Eight there is a poem which will clarify why I feel as I do.

"I can do all things through Christ which strengthens me." Philippians 4:13

3

Dealing with Grief
and Stress of Today

You might hate your life now and still be grieving. It is easy to lose one's self in grief. Grief is our response to loss: grief never ends, but it changes. In the meantime, we all need to take care of ourselves by eating right, getting some exercise and enough sleep. And no, I'm not going to tell you what to eat or give you a list of exercises; there are many books about this already. But I may tell you why you need to do these things. This chapter is about you and how to deal with grief and with stress.

Before I talk more about grief, I would like to tell you one more thing. Many widows commented that they dreaded the first anniversary of their husband's death. They were fearful that it would bring back all the bad memories of their loss. However, it seemed to me that the anticipation of the first anniversary was really worse than the actual day itself. Actually, the second anniversary of his death might be more difficult than the first. By that time reality has sunk in, but you may not have yet developed new goals or a meaningful purpose in life.

You all may have a different approach to that anniversary day when it comes around each year. This is true for any "death anniversary", not just you husband's. I find it a day to remember the good times. Sometimes I look at pictures of our years together; other times, I visit his grave at Arlington National Cemetery and sit there and tell him about my life and about our family happenings. I know some widows remark about the date or put a photo of their husband on Facebook and get a lot of uplifting comments from their friends. It is another day in your life. I think that your husband would appreciate being remembered but would not be happy that you were still sad and mournful. Contrarily, Jane Woods Shoemaker, author of <u>Widow's Walk</u> wrote, "Perhaps days of such significance are times to let down and let grief have its day. Those feelings of sorrow and despair are within you, so express them. Crying can be therapeutic to the mind and body."

GRIEF

Even as you grieve, you probably know that life must go on. In 1969, Elizabeth Kubler-Ross introduced the five stages of dying in her book <u>On Death and Dying</u>. Undoubtedly you are familiar with these stages. Before her death she and her co-author, grief expert David Kessler, adapted her stages for grief in their book, <u>On Grief and Grieving</u>. He writes that these stages help us learn to process and live with our loss. However, they are only guide lines and are not experienced in any specific order, since everyone will process grief differently.

You may go through all these stages, or just some, but in the end, you should find yourself accepting your loss. "You may never feel okay about the loss of a loved one, but you will accept the reality of it…and it is a permanent reality." states Dr. Kessler. In the meantime, be careful what you say to yourself; some thoughts can bring on depression. One widow wrote: "If you are saying negative things (or having negative thoughts), just stop yourself! Be terribly aware of what you are telling yourself. Give yourself positive self-talk."

The Harvard Women's Health Watch had an interesting article about grief in their December, 2016 issue. (volume 24, number 4). In "Getting Through Grief", the article identifies the normal process of grieving, which usually lasts from six to 12 months. Included in the process may be a yearning for the person, a deep sadness, memories of shared experiences, physical problems, lethargy, and emotional surges. In this article, Dr. Michael Craig Miller, Assistant Professor of Psychiatry at Harvard Medical School says, "There are cultural differences and personal style differences, but grief is a shared part of the human experience." He states that grief and depression are hard to tell apart, and if you are finding yourself overwhelmed by grief, you may want to seek help from a professional.

The following was written by a new widow, and perhaps you can identify with her feelings. "I lost my husband less than a year ago. He was my best friend, my partner, my lover and my world. He was my only boyfriend and we were married for 45 years. My children and friends help me the best they can, but they can't make the pain and heart break go away. They tell me to get out, find people to talk to or things to do. For me it's just not easy. There are days when I just sit and cry. I pray every night for help; so far it hasn't come. Unless you have lived through it, you don't know what it's like to be lonely and heart broken and trying to find something to replace those emotions."

For some widows, the normal process of grieving does descend into a prolonged depression. "Complicated grief" is a term used for this minority of women who suffer an unrelieved yearning that intrudes on everyday coping. Symptoms can include extreme focus on the loved one, intense longing or pining for the deceased and problems accepting the death. Their loss can be shattering, but this is not the norm. Most people are resilient. Almost every-one suffers, but humans are wired to do this suffering naturally.

This complicated grief syndrome was identified in the mid-nineties by Dr. Katherine Shear, Director of the Center for Complicated Grief at the Columbia School of Social Work. They can be con-tacted at 212-851-2107 or www.info@complicatedgrief.colum-bia.edu .

As stated, letting go of your grief entails starting to accept your husband's absence. "Thinking that he is much better off now than he was here, and that life is eternal gave me peace." One widow said, "Due to my spirituality and age, I always try to understand whatever situation is happening to me. Accept that death is a nor-mal thing of creation and that my role is to accept it and abandon myself to the grace of God. I remember my husband with all his good virtues and how much he loved me. I also remember all the good things we did and enjoyed together."

A suggestion I found most beneficial was for you to let people know what helps you. Too often, your friends don't know exactly how to act around you while you are grieving. They want to help and will be relieved if you tell them what they can do for you. Perhaps they can do your laundry or get groceries for you. Maybe they can just sit and hold your hand and listen or laugh with you over remembrances. It's also all right to let them know if you would prefer to be left alone.

GUILT VS. REGRET

Another consideration is that guilt and regret are often confused, which can complicate your healing. Guilt is caused by doing something that you knew was wrong. Those guilty feelings may grow and give way to depression.

Regret comes from thinking later you should have done something differently or better. Perhaps you keep thinking, 'If only I had...... (fill in the blank), the results would have been different.' This regret can easily change into self-blame and guilt. Shelly Webb, RN and founder of Intentional Caregiver says, "Regret can be summed up by exchanging it with the words I wish." The difference is that guilt felt when what you did intentionally is a negative feeling. Regret is more positive; you just wish you could change the past.

For years after my husband's death, I felt guilty that I had allowed the physician to convince me to transfer him from the hospital to a nursing home. She persuaded me that I couldn't care for him at home because of the oxygen and medications he was on. He was moved from the hospital to the nursing home on Friday. He died there on Saturday night. I felt guilty because I knew he had not wanted to end up in a nursing home. I still regret to this day that I didn't override her suggestion and bring him home to die. However, I have let go of my guilt.

"Guilt is probably the most painful companion to death."

...Elizabeth Kubler-Ross

Signs You are Getting Better

In the depths of mourning, you can't imagine things will ever get better, but slowly they do. There will be small changes at first... looking forward to seeing your grandchild or laughing at a joke. Initially you may feel guilty for this small moment of joy and begin to grieve again. But as the moments become more frequent, and you find your outlook changing, you'll probably notice the pace of recovery accelerating. Other signs you may notice:

- Memories are now a source of comfort...paging through a photo album or hearing a song you both loved brings a smile rather than tears.
- You can enjoy time alone without needing companionship to distract you from feeling sad and lonely.
- You start looking forward to the holidays or other occasions that used to evoke painful memories.

- You have stopped feeling exhausted all the time.
- Sometime can pass between reflections about your loved one.
- You can enjoy a good laugh without feeling guilty.
- You begin to make long-term plans for the future...you begin to move away from a one-day-at-a-time.
- You look forward to getting up each morning.
- You begin to accept things as they are and stop trying to return to the way things were.
- You can get lost in a book or movie.
- You no longer have to make daily or weekly trips to the cemetery.
- You feel confident again...the awkwardness or weakness you felt before is replaced with a new sense of self.
- The role that your loved one played in your life begins to be filled in by yourself and others.
- You can reach out to others going through a similar situation...compassion for others helps your own healing process.
- Your find small blessings to be grateful for...you start to appreciate the good things you still have in your life.

I can't take credit for the above "signs". They were listed in a very enlightening booklet from MOAA Info Exchange, (Military Officers Association of America). It is entitled "Turning the Corner; Surviving the Loss of a Loved One."

You may be experiencing some of these signs and realize you are growing and getting stronger. Several of the widows I talked to said, "Don't whine and complain about 'Poor me!' You should have a positive attitude." Well… you can cry if you want to, but you may feel better if you just remember the good times. However, as you know, that is just my opinion. As stated above, weeping can be therapeutic. But I prefer to remember what the Dalai Lama once said, "Just one small positive thought in the morning can change your whole day."

Every day may not be good, but there is good in every day. Eventually you'll find yourself comfortable in this new situation and on your way to independence. This can be true even for those of you who have never been independent. I'm talking about you who married your childhood sweetheart and went from parents' home to a husband and home without ever being in charge of your own life. Just remember that independence is good; self-pity has limitations. Learn how to be alone but not lonely; that is a key.

Adrea Cope, wrote an article I found on the internet entitled "The Difference Between Being Alone and Being Lonely". She wrote, "There is a magnificent difference between being lonely and being alone. Being lonely is that kind of aching that resonates in your chest. That dull, constant feeling that follows you around all day long. Typically, these feelings are most prominent after recently losing that person who make your world a little brighter."

Cope continues, "But being alone is a different situation completely. Being alone is a state of being; loneliness is a state of the mind. Being alone is sitting under a tree for an afternoon and reading a book and enjoying every single minute of it. It is doing things by yourself, but also doing them for yourself."

I had looked at the single swan swimming around the lake and thought, "How sad; she is alone." Generally, by summer there is a swan couple escorting this year's brood of cygnets around the lake. Then I remembered that I, too, am alone, but I'm not sad. And I'm not lonely. Then I thought maybe the swan isn't either. When I watch the beautiful sunset, or see a family of ducks cavorting around, I would like to share the scene with my husband, but it doesn't lessen the beauty of the scene. I can enjoy it all by myself.

Sometimes certain places bring peace to individuals. Perhaps you can find a place where you can go when you are feeling blue, a place where you can find peace, where you can be alone but not lonely. I have a 60-year-old swing that my father built on my back deck at home. I go there often to sit and regroup, to just remember the good times, or reflect on plans or solutions. Sometimes I sit there and read, or just watch the deer come out of the woods or the foxes carrying food for their young. It is so peaceful. To quote Adrea Cope again, "Being alone is an art; embrace it."

Yes, I have collected a lot of information for you to digest. But now, let's think about your health. These past months or years have probably been quite stressful for you, when you were expecting the worse, and eventually watching your husband die. You may not have been considering yourself and your health, but now is the time. When was the last time you saw a doctor? Have you been eating well and taking your vitamins? One widow's comments about eating, "Cook as little or as much as you enjoy doing but do be sure you eat healthy food. Treats are allowed. Grocery shopping can be a challenge for a onesie, but practice helps and grocery stores are accommodating." I'll write more about this in Chapter Four.

෬෨ ෬

STRESS

Perhaps you have not been taking very good care of yourself. I remember how it was when my husband was getting sicker; he was not improving; the prognosis was not good. I was concerned mainly about taking care of him and seeing that he had the best quality of life during this time.

He had such strength and integrity, right up to his death. Our daughter was engaged and the wedding was pending. He promised that he would be there to "walk her down the aisle", what every girl dreams of at her wedding. Unfortunately, he was hospitalized a week before the wedding, due to another stroke caused by the brain cancer, but he was there at the wedding. He was attired in his Army dress white uniform, the same one he had worn at our wedding 33 years ago, and he'd also worn at his other three children's weddings. He couldn't walk; he couldn't even hold his head up without help. But he "walked" her down the aisle holding her hand. He was sitting in a wheelchair that was pushed down the aisle by our son. It was a beautiful wedding. The newlyweds didn't want to go on their honey moon, but Dad insisted. Again, he promised he would be there when they got home. And he was. However, he died two days after they returned. He died with his daughter, his twin sister, and me at his bedside. Need I say this was a stressful time for me and for all our family?

We all have our stories, and no doubt we all have had stress in our own situations. So now, we must turn our attention to ourselves. I hope you are feeling a sense of expectation; a new strength to give yourself permission to do what you want. So, keep reading and perhaps you will learn something you don't know, something that will help you.

I can't think of a greater stress than losing someone you love, be it a husband, a child or even a beloved pet. Stress results from a "stressor", often an event or a worrisome subject, and your response to it. Actually, the death of a spouse is ranked number one as a "stressor" on the Stress Index Scale. A stressor can be significant, or relatively minor, states Dr. Joyce Johnson, a health care consultant in Chevy Chase, MD, "You can mitigate the actual stress---your subjective response to the stressor." Now, the death of a spouse is not a minor stress, so just taking a moment to reflect and decided whether it matters or whether you can do anything to change it doesn't work here. However, some suggestions to diminish stress have occurred to me.

Studies show that a good night's sleep can cure a lot of ills. Are you sleeping well? Ideally, one should get seven to eight hours of sleep nightly and if you are doing this, you have probably found that sleep helps to reduce stress. On the other hand, you don't want to sleep your life away. It is reported that more than nine hours of sleep constantly is not beneficial and can make you more lethargic. If you are having problems going to sleep, there are several tips about how to do so in the next chapter. Also, I have read that if you just can't get to sleep, you can get up and sit in a comfortable chair and read until you are sleepy. I do occasionally turn on the night light and read a few chapters in a book, if I can't sleep. I have never gotten up to read, however. You won't disturb anyone if you turn on the light and read in bed. Short daytime naps are also good, as long as you don't sleep the whole afternoon away, and then wonder why you can't sleep that night.

And, talking about naps, Rojo is presently asleep on her rug, practically surrounded by lovely but noisy, mallard ducks, some whom are taking a "cat nap" as well. Like me, she's a "senior" dog, and actually has more gray hair than I do. She does nap a lot, but for an eleven-year-old canine, she does well. She still loves to run around and chase squirrels. Keeping active is always good, for pets as well as for us. Walks for us…I imagine not many of us still "run". But back to stress.

Recalling that endings are new beginnings, the place to start is to take a good look at yourself. Several widows commented on appearances, that you should "keep yourself attractive" and your routine should include self-improvement. The 95-year-old widow said, "We all may differ in our ways of coping. Don't let yourself forget to keep up appearances. Dress each day as if you may go out to lunch unexpectedly. This adds up to continuing to enjoy getting new, pretty things to make you feel and look good." I like to get new clothes, but must admit, as I sit here writing in my "camping clothes," …shorts and top, I am definitely not dressed to go to lunch! Well, perhaps a picnic would be okay.

I am actually writing while sitting at a picnic table beside my lake. There is a lovely breeze blowing onshore and the birds are singing. My favorite swan just floated by. It's really not a hardship for me to spend all summer here writing this book! However, back to business. Well, one more thing. There is a big RV sitting across from me. On its side is written… "Stress, stress, stress…Stress Relief Vehicle," which I think implies that relaxation begins when you are parked here at the lake. Stress relief…this is what we are all aiming for.

Your body reacts to stress in many ways. Immediately after your spouse's death, you may be in shock, and experience what is entitled "brain fog". It isn't a medical condition itself, but rather a symptom. It's a type of cognitive dysfunction involving memory problems, lack of mental clarity, poor concentration and inability to focus. It doesn't have to be a permanent fixture in your life… it is caused by stress. This is only one symptom of stress. See the list below.

The American Institute of Stress (AIS) has complied the following list entitled "Stress Effects". (This list is printed with permission from AIS. For further information contact: American Institute of Stress, 9112 Camp Bowie West Blvd. #228, Fort Worth, TX 76116 phone: 682-239-6823 www.stress.org)

50 Common Signs and Symptoms of Stress

1. Frequent headaches, jaw clenching or pain
2. Gritting, grinding teeth
3. Stuttering or stammering
4. Tremors, trembling of lips, hands
5. Neck ache, back pain, muscle spasms
6. Light headedness, fainting, dizziness
7. Ringing, buzzing or "popping" sounds
8. Frequent blushing, sweating

9. Cold or sweaty hands, feet
10. Dry mouth, problems swallowing
11. Freequent colds, infections, herpes sores
12. Rashes, itching, hives, "goose bumps"
13. Unexplained or frequent "allergy" attacks
14. Heartburn, stomach pain, nausea
15. Excess belching, flatulence
16. Constipation, diarrhea, loss of control
17. Difficulty breathing, frequent sighing
18. Sudden attacks of life threatening panic
19. Chest pain, palpitations, rapid pulse
20. Frequent urination
21. Diminished sexual desire or performance
22. Excess anxiety, worry, guilt, nervousness
23. Increased anger, frustration, hostility
24. Depression, frequent or wild mood swings
25. Increased or decreased appetite
26. Insomnia, nightmares, disturbing dreams
27. Difficulty concentrating
28. Trouble learning new information
29. Forgetfulness, disorganization, confusion
30. Difficulty in making decisions
31. Feeling overloaded or overwhelmed
32. Frequent crying spells or suicidal thoughts
33. Feelings of loneliness or worthlessness
34. Little interest in appearance, punctuality
35. Nervous habits, fidgeting, feet tapping
36. Increased frustration, irritability, edginess
37. Overreaction to petty annoyances
38. Increased number of minor accidents

39. Obsessive or compulsive behavior
40. Reduced work efficiency or productivity
41. Lies or excuses to cover up poor work
42. Rapid or mumbled speech
43. Excessive defensiveness or suspiciousness
44. Problems in communication, sharing
45. Social withdrawal and isolation
46. Constant tiredness, weakness, fatigue
47. Frequent use of over-the-counter drugs
48. Weight gain or loss without diet
49. Increased smoking, alcohol or drug use
50. Excessive gambling or impulse buying

Wow! This is quite a list. Just keep in mind that everyone feels stress at one time or another and that not all stress is bad. Sometimes stress keeps you on your toes and doing your best. However, if you have checked off an abundance of the above, you have more than a little stress. If your stress level is so high that you are having problems functioning, perhaps you should stop reading now and make an appointment with a medical professional!

The good news is that you can do something about stress. Greg Fricchione, MD, Director of the Benson-Henry Institute for Mind Body Medicine at Massachusetts General Hospital says, "There are a number of effective strategies that individuals can use on their own to reduce stress and buffer themselves against its debilitating effect." Dr. Fricchione has seven strategies that are effective ways to cope with stress, minimize its effects on daily life, and recover from setbacks. He suggests: walk away if you can, cultivate optimism, take decisive action, protect your body, work out regularly, don't isolate, and harness the relaxation response. "These techniques give you brain a respite from constant tension and break the chain of everyday thought," Dr. Fricchione says. "Through them, you can achieve a state of deep rest that alters your physical and emotional reactions to stress." (Mind, Mood, and Memory, Volume 15G-T www. mindmoodandmemory.com)

I find one of the best stress relivers is to exercise. Any type of exercise is good, from yoga to workouts at the YMCA or gym lifting weights and doing aerobic exercises. You may choose to swim, play tennis, or just take walks. If you have a dog you will be required to walk at least twice a day. You know how I enjoy my Irish Setter, and pets can help one relax and reduce stress. Even if you don't like to exercise, find some activity that you do like and put it on your to-do daily list. Some prefer to garden instead and that really is an exercise in itself. I don't think knitting is enough of an exercise, however.

I can't presume to give you all the answers on how to "de-stress". I can, however, offer some suggestions and do have my own list of stress relievers. Aren't you glad to discover that there are so many ways you can reduce your level of stress?

PATI'S LIST OF STRESS RELIEVERS

- Meditate…yoga, tai chi, breathing techniques
- Warm bath…with lots of bubbles
- Message…by masseuse or self-giving scalp or foot message
- Herbal teas
- Get more sleep…don't eat or exercise late in evening

- Organize your belongings …clutter can cause an increase in stress
- Exercise…did I hide this well?
- Aromatherapy…smell of fresh bakes chocolate chip cookies, scented candles, popular oils or lotions…all are lovely
- Hobbies
- Nature walk, or just sit in your swing or lawn chair and look around
- Music…listen or make your own. Sing if you can carry a tune…or not
- Laughing at something every day. Belly laughs are wonderful!
- Journaling, write it all down…call it your "Stress Diary"
- Pray
- Family support is always good
- Just say "No." …to something you don't want to do
- Just say "Yes!" …to something you do
- Eat a diet of healthy foods, decrease the "junk food"…but treats are okay
- Gratitude…focus on blessings and things that go right
- Read a good book

Another way to relieve stress is to watch the swan and four baby ducks who are wandering around my table looking for corn. They are adorable! I've already mentioned that resorts like Wilderness are a great place to relax and decrease your stress level.

"I'm too blessed to be stressed!"

4

You...Still on the Right Side of the Grass

Here you are with your life to live, and you must take care of yourself! Forgive me for using this as a title for this chapter. My husband, when he was getting sicker daily, would wake up and comment, "Well, I'm still on the right side of the grass today!" ...then we would both laugh and get on with the day. He is no longer here, but I am and have my own life to live. And to you I say, "Welcome to the rest of your life! You have a new beginning." Let's see how long you may live.

LONGEVITY

Now that you know what to do about stress, I'll move on to other possible problems you might (or might not) encounter. Today the average life expectancy for all Americans is 78.6 years; women's life expectancy is 81.1 years and for men it is 76.1 years. If you are brave enough and want to find out what your estimated life expectancy is, go to the website www.mylifecalc.net and answer the list of questions. Your life expectancy will show up on a gauge. They suggest you try adjusting your answers to see how lifestyle changes will affect your longevity.

Americans don't have the highest life expectancy in the world. Googling this, I found that many other countries have a higher rate. Countries that have the highest quality of life tend to have the longest-living citizens, says the Central Intelligence Agency, which has tracked the average life expectancy for every country in the world. Countries in the "listed" top ten include Japan, Switzerland, Singapore, Australia, Spain, Iceland, Italy, Israel, Sweden and France. The United States ranks 37th out of the 191 countries on that list. Before you start thinking that perhaps you should move to another country, remember that the global expectancy average in 2015 was 71.4 years. Approximately five percent of humanity is American, and with our average life expectancy of 78.6 years, we aren't doing so bad. (World population is over 7.6 billion!)

But since I am throwing around numbers, you may be wondering what the population of the United States is. The estimated USA population was over 325 million by September, 2017. Statistics show there are approximately 13.6 million widowed persons in the United States and 80% are widows! That is almost 11 million women! The nearly 800,000 women who lose their husbands each year will be widows for an average of 14 years, according to the US Bureau of Census. Does it make you feel any better to know that you are not alone? It appears that widowhood is a very common experience in the life cycle of contemporary Americans. Women are more likely than men to be widowed, since women live longer than men, and wives are generally younger than their husband. However, even if your health is good now, it may not be all clear sailing. The following are some potential health problems you may encounter as you age.

POTENTIAL HEALTH PROBLEMS

It is predicted that by 2020 one in every five Americans will be 65 or older. This population is now called the "Senior Tsunami" ...or is it the "Silver Tsunami"? I can't remember, since it's been awhile since I was just 65! However, if you are a "senior citizen" here are some potential problems you should be aware of.

1. Osteoporosis: As one ages, the body begins to absorb bone cells more quickly than new bone cells can be made causing bones to become thinner and weaker. This is generally more a problem for females than for males, since men have stronger bones to begin with. Ladies with a small frame and slight build also have bones that are less dense, which makes them more vulnerable. Less dense bones become fragile and break more easily, therefore, if one falls a fracture is more likely to occur. These fractures generally occur in the hips, wrists, or spine. There are no symptoms for this disease. However, bone density tests can be done periodically to measure bone loss. This test is called a DEXA scan (Dual-energy x-ray absorptiometry). It is today's established standard for measuring bone mineral density. A less severe loss of bone density is called osteopenia.

   There are a number of treatments available for osteoporosis. If you are diagnosed as having decreased bone density check with your physician to find the best treatment for you. Your primary care physician may refer you to an endocrinologist who specializes in osteoporosis.

The "ABCD of bone health" is an easy way to remember what you need to do for healthy bones. The A stands for activity, B for balance, C for calcium and D for Vitamin D.

Considering activities, only weight-bearing exercises help to strengthen bones. This means exercises that put strain on your muscles, such as running, jumping, walking, practicing yoga, and even walking up and down stairs. Unfortunately, swimming and biking are not considered methods for bone strengthening. In women, muscle mass is strongly linked to bone strength at the hips, lumbar (lower) spine, and tibia (leg) bone as well as the bones in the forearms. These are the bones more likely to be fractured in a fall. It is advisable to do some strengthening training like weight-lifting regularly. Now don't fret. I promised in Chapter Three that I wouldn't give you exercises, didn't I? Well, please forgive me. You don't need to join a gym or get a trainer. All you need is a five-pound weight you can buy at Walmart, a search on the internet for the exercise program and you are good to go. If you are unsure of what exercises to do, you can always consult a physical therapist or a physical fitness consultant, or join an exercise class. (See, I am not telling you what exercises to do.)

However, a large multiyear study by Preventive Medicine Research Institute found that people's telomeres, the parts of our DNA that get shorter as we age, were significantly longer in those who exercised often when compared with those who were sedentary.

In case you are wandering what telomeres are, I looked it up so you won't have to. Telomeres, the part of chromosomes that affect aging, are the protective "caps" on the cells at the ends of your DNA. They shorten with age, but there are steps you can take to slow down this aging process. These telomeres do matter because they enable your cells to reproduce so you can heal, grow and thrive. Every time our cells divide a tiny bit of your telomere, which protect your genetic information, is used up. Years of clinical data support the link between telomere length and the aging process. I gleaned this information from the Telomere Learning Center. (www.teloyears.com) They have a "simple genetic test that reveals your cellular age" available for purchase. It is a good idea to keep your telomeres as long as possible for as long as possible!

It is also thought that calcium and Vitamin D3 consumption are important when considering osteoporosis. Again, although I am not prescribing, please discuss the intake of both with your physician. However, not getting enough calcium and vitamin D3 could put bones at risk. It is suggested that up to age 50 you should get 1,000 milligrams (mg) of calcium daily and after 50 this should be increased to 1,200 mg. A lot of foods have calcium; it is found in milk, yogurt, broccoli and calcium fortified foods. If you don't eat these foods, you can get calcium from a good calcium vitamin supplement. The body absorbs only 500-600 mg of calcium at one time, so spread your supplements throughout the day.

Note: new research shows calcium supplements may raise the risk of heart attacks and kidney stones. This is also something you should discuss with your doctor.

Vitamin D3, the "sunshine vitamin", is a fat-soluble vitamin that is essential for the absorption of calcium. You need 600 International Units (IU) daily if under age 70, which increases to 800 IU if over 70. (Perhaps they think older folk don't go out in the sun as much?) Whatever! You still should use sunscreen when out in the sun. Yes, it blocks UVB light, which theoretically means less vitamin D is absorbed. However, few people put on enough sunscreen to block all UVB light, or use sunscreen irregularly, so sunscreen's effects on vitamin D might not be that important.

2. Macular degeneration: Macular Degeneration is a serious threat to the sight and those over 75 have a 30% risk of developing it. The macula, located in the back of the eye, is the part of the eye that allows you to see fine details. If you are in the early stages of age-related macular degeneration, you may not have any symptoms. The first sign you may notice is a gradual change in the quality of your vision or find that straight lines appear distorted to you. This may gradually turn into a dramatic loss of your central vision. Since this has no immediate symptoms, it is wise to schedule regular eye exams with your ophthalmologist.

    There are two types, wet and dry macular degeneration. The dry is the most common type, but if the disease progresses to the point that the blood vessels begin to leak into the retina; it's known as wet macular degeneration. The wet is more serious and causes more vision loss. When diagnosed early, you can take vitamins containing antioxidants lutein and zeaxanthin which can apparently slow the progression. One of the most common is Bausch and Lomb Preser Vision AREDS2. Your ophthalmologist will tell you what is best for you.

3. <u>Glaucoma</u>: is another age-related health problem affecting your vision. Glaucoma causes an increase in the fluid of your eye which can gradually damage the optic nerve that connects the retina in the eye to the brain. Again, there are no symptoms initially, but it causes a loss of peripheral vision and eventually your total vision may become affected. Glaucoma can be treated with daily drops which your ophthalmologist will prescribe, or with laser treatment. My mother had glaucoma and used the drops twice daily for years. Since my research shows that genetic factors play a role in glaucoma, I actually had a laser procedure done twenty years ago to prevent glaucoma. It is painless and takes only a few moments and you can forget about getting glaucoma.

I'm not even going to elaborate about cataracts, because they are so common that everyone knows all about them. Surgery can correct cataracts, so generally, they aren't really an "eye problem" for seniors.

4. <u>Hearing loss</u>: Forty-three percent of Americans over 65 will lose the ability to hear high-pitched sounds. This is called presbycusis. Since I am not a fan of violins, I don't really care! However, persons with a history of loud sound exposure (think military artillery, loud music, or construction noises) also can experience a greater hearing loss in later years. The consonants are harder to hear as well as softer voices of women and children. This is why hearing tests are necessary. You might require a hearing aid. Do you find yourself saying "What?"… a lot?

5. <u>Cognitive Impairment</u>: This is a fairly common age-related memory loss and its chance of it occurring is 68% if you

are 65 or older. Since that figure seemed rather high, I did more research. Mild cognitive impairment (MCI) occurs with a slight but noticeable and measurable decline in cognitive abilities, including memory and thinking skills, but doesn't jeopardize independent living. As we age, it's normal to forget minor details; it's a part of the aging process. (Think "senior moments.") However, if you become forgetful, and confused when doing tasks such as paying bills or following multiple-step directions, perhaps you should see your doctor. Once cognitive impairments become more severe than what's normal based on age, this is considered to be MCI. A person with MCI is at an increased risk of developing Alzheimer's or another dementia.

It might make you feel better to know that MCI overlaps with both normal age-related cognitive impairments and the onset of Alzheimer's. Keep in mind that not everyone who suffers from MCI will develop Alzheimer's, but those who are eventually diagnosed with Alzheimer's first suffered from MCI.

6. Alzheimer's Disease: (AD) This is a brain disease that erodes the ability to remember and think clearly, eventually rendering the person unable to perform the basic tasks. It is the most common form of dementia and 70% of patients are those aged 70 or over. This is an irreversible, progressive disease of the brain. There are many scientists working on curing this disease and let's hope they will find a cure before we ourselves need one.

Please note...everybody forgets things occasionally and it does not mean you are getting dementia. Memory lapses are a normal occurrence with age. Just because you forget where you left your keys or your phone does not mean you have symptoms of Alzheimer's! If one didn't "forget" things, just think how crowded your brain would be! (I actually heard something about this on the radio. They are doing tests to prove that we forget things so that we can learn other things!) When memory losses impair your ability to function independently in your home, or if your family and friends notice a change in your abilities or behavior, these may be signs or symptoms of dementia. Other symptoms include language problems, disorientation, and face-recognition issues. Even then memory loss doesn't automatically mean you have Alzheimer's. Memory loss can be a symptom of at least 75 different medical conditions. (Now, don't start worrying about this!!!) Only five percent of people aged 65 to 74 have Alzheimer's. The younger you are the more likely a memory related issue is something other than Alzheimer's. Just think… as long as we worry about getting Alzheimer's, it is most likely we don't have it! It is when we actually have the symptoms of Alzheimer's that we stop worrying. I don't know how this works, but it does make sense.

Note: If you have a family member who has AD, know that six in ten sufferers wander, which is a serious safety risk. You can get an electronic tracking device which will alert you when he starts to wander. (MedicAlert Alzheimer's Association Safe Return 888-572-8566 www.alz.org)

I'm sure everyone has gone to get something in another room and then when arriving forgotten what it is you were after.

The trick is to go back through the last doorframe and bin-go...you will remember. (This forgetfulness is just a trick your brain does to get you to do more exercise. It's called "doorway duh?")

Tips: Have a certain place where you always put your keys, so they don't end up left in the door or in some other crazy location. Keep your land line so you can call your cell phone when it is missing. Of course, the cell phone has to be charged, so get into the habit of plugging it in routinely every night. This problem is making me worry a bit! I am constantly forgetting where I last used my cell phone. Fortunately, I still have a land line and can call my cell phone if I just can't locate it...if it has power.

If you are interested in being involved in Alzheimer's research, you can contact the Alzheimer Association at www.alz.org or email info@alz.org. The Alzheimer Association Trial match program is a free clinical study matching service that connects individuals with Alzheimer's, caregivers, and healthy volunteers to current studies. Their motto is "Don't just hope for a cure. Help us find one."

KNOW THE TEN SIGNS

This is probably a good place to say that early detection matters with Alzheimer's Disease. The following ten signs of this disease are taken from a publication from the Alzheimer's Association, and who should know them better?

- Memory loss that disrupts daily life
- Challenges in planning or solving problems

- Difficulty completing familiar tasks
- Confusion with time or place
- Trouble understanding visual images and spatial relationships
- New problems with words in speaking or writing
- Misplacing things and losing the ability to retrace steps
- Decreased or poor judgment
- Withdrawal from work or social activities
- Changes in mood and personality

If you want more information, the Alzheimer's Association number is: 800-272-3900 or web address: www.alz.org

7. Incontinence: How many recognize this one? This is a problem older woman, usually over 50, must sometimes deal with. This occurs because pelvic muscles lose strength with age and become less able to control the bladder. Some women, after childbearing, will have a prolapsed uterus, which causes pressure on the bladder thus leading to incontinence. This is a problem that can be controlled or even cured... says the physical therapist in me. I told you I wouldn't talk about exercises, but this one is so good and really easy to do. It's called the Kegel exercise and is sort of vaginal "pushups". It really does strengthen those muscles in the pelvic floor around the urethra and gives you more control over the "bladder flow." I would tell my patient to practice when sitting on the toilet by stopping the flow of urine. When you learn how to do this exercise, you can do it anytime and you must try to do at least 30-40 Kegels a day to get results. If this explanation is not clear, make an appointment with a physical therapist who can teach you.

Note: I think it is Maxine who considers it multitasking to be able to laugh and pee at the same time. You can wear mini-pads in your underwear if incontinence is a constant problem. However, I have heard that body scanners at airports sometimes "see" this pad and that will cause the agent to do a more thorough examination.

8. Arthritis: As we get older, it's normal to feel "stiff" in the mornings when you get out of bed. This does not mean you have arthritis. However, arthritis is a very common condition that one in six Americans will experience when the lining (cartilage) and fluid in some joint wears out, causing the bones to scrape against each other and cause increased pain. Osteoarthritis (OA) occurs in the larger joints such as the knees and hips. If you experience prolonged joint pain with joints that are swollen, red, and feel hot to touch, you may have rheumatoid arthritis (RA). This is a disease in which your immune system attacks your joints; it generally occurs in the smaller joints of the hands but can strike any joint, including the knees, wrists, neck, shoulders, elbows, feet, hips and even the jaw. There are seven factors that can increase your risk for RA: genetics, environment, smoking, gender, reproductive and breastfeeding history, age and ethnicity. Three-fourths of RA patients are women who have never given birth and the risk increases as one ages. It is highest in your 60's. Also, American Indians and Alaskan natives have higher incidences of RA.

There are many treatments for arthritis and, if physical therapy or medications don't work, you can get a total hip replacement, a total knee replacement, or shoulder replacement.

9. Balance Problems: Eight million Americans have significant problems with balance. Two-point-four million have chronic dizzy spells which are usually caused by inner ear problems. Medications or other medical problems can also cause balance problems. If you don't have these problems, but you balance is sometimes "off" there are many exercises which can help improve your balance. A lot of them are really fun! Again, I would suggest seeing a physical therapist who will teach you these exercises. This will make you feel steadier on your feet and help prevent falls. Your therapist can also give you suggestions to increase safety in your home, such as removing loose throw rugs which could cause you to trip, putting an extra handle beside a step or near the bathtub, and having good lighting. (Maybe I'll add a section about safety in the home later.)

Tips: These are good to remember: I promised my PT daughter I would always hold the railing when I went down the stairs to prevent losing my balance and possibly falling. Also, when you feel dizzy, it helps if you put your feet on the floor. This can also help decrease your dizziness. (I guess it gives your brain an assist to know which end is up?)

I will also add these comments from another widowed friend. She wrote, "To whatever ability you have, do try to stand erect and to carry yourself as tall as possible. Try not to shuffle but pick up your steps. However, do be careful and do be watchful, no quick turns. Be thoughtful about each action…being slower is okay." Erect posture and picking up your feet lest you trip on that rug is important to remember, but making quick turns is the main culprit here. If you turn too quickly, there is a chance you will lose your balance and fall... possibly with a resultant hip fracture! Statistics show that hip fractures can lead to an earlier death. It is the hip fracture itself that ultimately leads to death in these women! By all means...slow is okay!

Just for fun, I'm going to give you a few ideas that you can do throughout the day to help improve your balance. These are not exercises! While brushing your teeth, try to balance on one foot for 10-30 seconds; then switch feet. If that becomes too easy, try moving your leg to the side or back while still balancing on the opposite foot. When standing talking on the phone, march in place for a while, or side step. And one more, although this is not specifically to aid balance...whenever you sit or stand up from a chair, try to do it with your legs only; don't use your arms. If you do these ten times a day, you have done ten "squats" and you don't even know it!

If your balance is poor and you are at risk of falling, there are assistive devices that can help improve your balance, provide support and keep you mobile. Don't let your pride keep you from using one of the devices that can increase your safety and stability when walking. Trekking poles are often used for hiking. (I use them myself.) They can provide stability, help to improve your posture, balance and coordination.

Canes come in many varieties now and some standard canes are decorated with flowers, red hats or other interesting and colorful themes. People will notice this and perhaps comment instead of thinking that you are using a cane. If you need more support, there are also many varieties of walkers, some with wheels and even seats which come in handy when you are fatigued…or go to a grandchild's game and there are no seats available.

Again, I recommend your visit a PT to find out what is the best device for you if you feel a bit wobblily on your feet.

10. <u>Constipation</u>: Constipation is considered a problem if you have less than three bowel movements a week. It is caused by the colon absorbing too much water from food passing through and stools becoming hard, dry and difficult to pass. There can be many causes for this, including lack of fiber in your diet, lack of physical exercises or activity, or dehydration. There are medications, of course, which will help alleviate this problem, but first try to improve your diet, exercise and water consumption to see it that helps first. Of course, chronic constipation calls for another appointment with your physician.

And this period of your life is called the "Golden Years"? I haven't even addressed cancer, diabetes, heart disease and other serious disease, and I don't plan to. I think we need a bit of levity now, so we can lighten up! This is a poem I've seen frequently. I even saw it on a T-shirt one time! There are many different versions, but I like this one the best. It turns out that after all, we are not old…we are recycled teenagers!

Seenager

I've discovered my age group!
I'm a SEENAGER (Senior Teenager)
I have everything I wanted as a teenager,
only 50-60 years later.
I don't have to go to school or work.

I get an allowance every month.
I have my own pad.
I don't have a curfew.
I have my driver's license and my own car.
I have an ID that gets me into bars and the wine store.
I like the wine store the best.

The people I hang around with are not scared
of getting pregnant.
They aren't scared of anything.
They have been blessed this long, why be scared?
And, I don't have acne.

Brains of older people are slow because they know so much.
People do not decline mentally with age,
it just takes them longer to recall facts because
they have more information in their brains.
Scientists believe this also makes your hard of hearing
as it puts pressure on your inner ear.

Also, older people often go to another room to get something.
When they get there, they stand there wondering what they came for.

It is not a memory problem, it is nature's way of making
older people do more exercise.
So there!

I have friends to send this to but right now
I can't remember their names.
So please tell your friends;
they may be my friends too.

Don't you wish you had written this? It just points out that
laughter is good. So, go ahead, do something silly and then laugh
at yourself! Even if you do something silly or "stupid" without
meaning to, laugh anyway. Life is boring if one doesn't laugh.
Plus, laughing is good exercise. It's like jogging on the inside.
Laughter is also a great stress reliever!

TALK ABOUT FOOD

But back to becoming a healthier you. I know that you have heard
the benefits of eating a balanced diet with lots of fruits and vegetables. The "perfect plate" contains 50% fruits and vegetables,
25% whole grains, and 25% protein. Half of us older Americans
don't get enough protein. This could lead to many health concerns. Many diets are also deficient in calcium and fiber. Calcium
has been discussed in its relationship to osteoporosis, but in addition, a high percentage of Americans don't get enough magnesium, which is a mineral that allows the body to absorb calcium.
Who knew?

But I guess most of us do know that we should get the recommended 20-35 grams of dietary fiber per day. Furthermore, researchers at Harvard University say that Omega-3 deficiency is the 6th biggest health threat to Americans. Omega-3 are good fats, essential to not only your energy, but also to your life! You might want to talk to a nutritionist or dietician to be sure you are getting the right nutrition daily.

There are many cook books that give menus when cooking for one. Or, you can cook the amount you are used to and freeze one serving for later. Even if you don't feel like cooking, you can make delicious smoothies with fruits, some protein powder, ice and milk. (However, sometimes just eat the fruits and vegetables instead of making smoothies all the time. There is very little fiber in smoothies, compared to the actual fruits and vegetables.)

Lactose-intolerance can increase with age so if milk doesn't agree with you or you don't like it, there are wonderful "milk substitutes" in the dairy cases. There's almond milk, cashew milk, soy milk, rice milk, coconut milk, hemp milk...did I miss your favorite plant-based milk? I don't blame the Dairy Institute for complaining about these "foods" being called milk because they don't come from cows, but they do taste good. However, you might want to read the labels because the sweetened and flavored varieties have extra calories and sugar. They vary in protein content, as well as calories, so be selective. (As a senior, I require 45-47 grams of protein and should have less than 25 grams or 6 teaspoons, of sugar daily.) With organic milk, the calcium can "settle to the bottom" so be sure to shake it prior to pouring. If you want more information about plant-based milk, Google "7 Non-Dairy Milk Options" at www.goodhousekeeping.com .

MALNUTRITION

If you have only scanned the above paragraphs, and aren't really too interested in food, you may be at risk for malnutrition. Dietitian Fran Grossman, a nutrition counselor at Mount. Sinai Hospital, says that this is worrying because inadequate nutrition can affect brain function and increase your risk of osteoporosis, fractures, and other debilitation conditions. She also states, "Information on an older adult's eating patterns can be a useful red flag indicating their potential risk for deteriorating health and mortality." Granted, eating well is a challenge for seniors because as we age our sense of smell and taste diminish, which affects our enjoyment of foods, and as we age, our ability to absorb nutrients from food also diminishes. (We have already talked about the difficulty of "shopping, cooking and eating for one".)

Tip: you can increase your daily protein intake by eating peanut butter…now who doesn't like peanut butter? I sometimes eat a spoonful that is rolled in raisins…protein and iron intake. You can also add grated cheese on vegetables and put into soups and on sandwiches. Perhaps you can use herbs and spices to add life to bland foods. Of course, you can always talk to your doctor about taking vitamins, if you are not "eating right." Or perhaps you can go to a nutritionist for more information.

FIVE FOODS YOU SHOULD NEVER EAT

There are some interesting ideas on the Internet. Actually, there are numerous postings about "foods you should never eat". The following I found informative and interesting but you can form your own opinions. I picked five of the most common foods we eat daily.

1. The first was orange juice concentrate. Apparently, a lot of them have too much added sugars. I guess it is okay to drink "pure" orange juice that is not made from concentrate. I remember drinking many glasses of concentrated OJ when I was younger. I can still see that pitcher my mother used to mix the frozen concentrate with water. Perhaps it is just better to eat the whole orange. That way you will get some of that necessary fiber in your diet.

2. Margarine is also on the "never eat list" because of the trans fats it contains. Trans fats are never good; they increase your LDL, the bad cholesterol. I like butter better than margarine even if it has saturated fat. My body knows how to digest it. Do you remember that during World War II margarine was white with a little capsule of yellow coloring that you mixed with it to make it look like butter?

3. Now this one is a shocker, because of all the publicity you hear about eating "whole wheat" bread...another food on the lists. Be sure you buy 100% whole wheat bread. If it isn't 100% whole wheat, it can contain white enriched flour, which gives you a "sugar spike and crash" without any nutritional value. Basically, enriched flour means nutrients are stripped from

the bread (and then added later?) Fiber-rich breads that are 100% whole wheat contain vitamins B6 and E, magnesium, zinc, folic acid and chromium…all of which are good for you. So…the "less than 100% whole wheat" is the culprit here.

(Whole grain can be a mix of many grains, or just the grain you prefer. The only caveat is that while wheat products usually have only one gram of fiber as opposed to the two grams or more that other whole grains contain. Some other whole grains are oatmeal, rye, rice, barley, buckwheat.)

4. Number four is processed soy. This is very controversial topic! Some say it is a "wonderful superfood" or conversely, a "hormone disruption poison", depending on whom you are talking to. It appears that processing the soy, also known as soy protein isolate, has none of the of carbs, fat or fiber that makes soy so healthy. Soy protein isolate is added to a lot of products. Whole organic soy that hasn't been so processed is considered a better source of protein. The Japanese people thrive on it. They use fermented soy which is good for you; it contains probiotics, and Vitamin K2 which help build strong bones and supports brain health. I did a lot of research on soy and even the Federal Drug Administration (FDA) agent I talked to declined to comment if processed soy was good for you or not. He did say that the FDA doesn't object to soy being in foods. I guess you should talk to a nutritionist or just form your own opinion.

5. Corn is apparently listed here because much of the corn produced in the United States is a GMO. This stands for Genetically Modified Organism. A GMO is an organism

whose genome has been altered by the techniques of genetic engineering so that its DNA contains one or more genes not normally found there. The purpose of GMO is to develop crops with pest-resistant traits and possibly improve nutritional content. However, these GMO products are banned in France, Italy, Germany and many other countries. GMO foods are found in lots of products, but the FDA requires that the package be labeled when they are present. I believe this is true...when I called the FDA and the agent wouldn't talk about soy, but he did comment that GMO foods must be identified.

If I have really confused you, this may help. Dr. Mehmet Oz, Oprah's favorite doctor, has a "rule of five" that makes a lot of sense. He lists 5 ingredients you should never eat:

- High fructose corn sugar
- Sugar
- "Enriched" products
- Trans fats
- Saturated fats

He explains the reasons why these foods should be avoided on his YouTube presentation dated 8/21/2014. I think I could pretty much avoid all these except sugar. Must admit I do have a "sweet tooth".

MORE ABOUT GMO

More research on GMO foods showed that a lot of products grown in the United States are genetically engineered! In fact, I called the Nestle Company to inquire about the Nestle Raisinets because on the package it is marked "gluten free" but also marked "partially produced with genetic engineering." When I inquired about what part of the dark chocolate covered raisins made with real fruit was genetically engineered, I was told that most corn, sugar cane, canola or soy grown here were GMO crops. (Nestle Company 800-258-6728. The lovely lady who politely answered all my questions said that they were available 24/7 to answer inquiries.) I must add that the Raisinets are very tasty. I might be addicted to them even though they contain GMO sugar and soy lecithin. In addition, it is rumored that they are good at raising the iron level in your blood. (Rumors are not always true.)

Of course, you can make your own decisions. Looks like it would be pretty difficult to omit all foods that have "ingredients that are not that good for you." However, we are fortunate today to have all this information on our food packages. It's a good idea to read what they say before you buy the product. Many processed and packaged foods contain added sugars. Have you heard that "fat-free foods" add sugar also? In addition, many dairy products contain carrageenan, a cheap thickening agent which is linked to gastrointestinal ulcers and cancer. It is also suggested that you eliminate foods with this ingredient. It's sad to know that certain foods you may be eating can make you "less than healthy." I guess the rule of thumb is to eat foods that are fresh, whole and not processed. Do you think a chocolate bar is considered "processed"? What would we do without chocolate???

I do remember being told that you should shop "around the outside of the grocery aisles, where the natural and fresh foods generally are, and avoid the inside isles that are full of processed foods." A good idea to remember?

(The FDA is requiring new food labels that will go into effect July 26, 2018. This labeling will include "added sugars" so you will know how much total sugar is in the product.)

Tip: Don't forget to bring your glasses or a magnifying glass when you go shopping. A lot of the print on the labels is very small.

STOP OR MODERATE

I probably don't have to mention smoking in this paragraph. You have undoubtedly been told what smoking does to your lungs, but has anyone mentioned that smoking also causes an increase in facial wrinkles? There is also a connection between smoking and a loss of memory. Research shows that a person who stops smoking has less cognitive decline that a person who continues to smoke.

And alcohol? One of the campers nearby has a little flag that says "Wine a bit, you'll feel better!" and I laugh every time I walk by. Apparently drinking alcohol can be helpful or harmful; it depends on how much you drink. Research suggests that moderate drinking reduces the risk of dementia. However, moderation is the key. Because of the biological difference between men and women, women are always more at risk of cognitive impairment and falls when they over imbibe. I'm talking about binge drinking which studies show is increasing in women over 60! Moderation means no more than two alcoholic drinks per day for a man and only one alcoholic drink per day for a woman. (One drink is usually considered to be 12 ounces of beer, 5 ounces of wine or 1½ ounces of hard liquor.) And no, moderation does not mean you can save a weeks' worth of wine for a Saturday night binge!

Still talking about moderation, it is advisable to go easy on the salt. Salt (sodium) is a mineral that helps control your body's fluid balance. It also helps send nerve impulses and affects muscle function. Too much sodium causes the body to excrete calcium and we've already covered that. Salt can also cause other problems such as edema and damage to the heart, aorta, and kidneys. However, some salt is necessary for your body to function properly. It is suggested that the daily amount of salt seniors consume should be less than 1500 milligrams (mg)a day. That's a bit more than ½ a teaspoon. (½ teaspoon = 1,150 mg, ¾ teaspoon = 1,725 mg and 1 teaspoon = 2,300 mg). However, since the rules keep changing, it is good to discuss this with your physician.

I looked up how much salt was in potato chips and found that plain chips have 170-185 mg/ounce. My favorite, sour cream and onion chips, have 180-205 mg/ounce. An ounce of chips is not very many! The small individual bag is generally 2-3 ounces. If you eat a whole bag or two, ...and how many have the discipline to stop at one or two chips? That provides a lot of your "recommended" salt allowance for the day!! However, relief... I then read that the daily optimal consumption of salt is 2,300 mg., as long as you are generally healthy. But it was suggested that people with high blood pressure should reduce their salt consumption to 1,500 mg daily. So many things to remember. Maybe I should dig up some ways to improve your memory.

Note: The majority of our salt intake comes from packaged and restaurant foods.

❧

AGING VS GETTING OLD

Birthdays are good. Each one means that you have lived another year. Enjoy each birthday; as you know, not everyone gets that opportunity. I understand that getting older is something that happens to everyone who lives long enough and keeps breathing. Aging is another issue. We all have to get older every year as the number counts up, however, we all don't age at the same rate. Some people look older than their age, yet others look a lot younger than the years say they are. The difference between aging and getting older is a state of mind. Getting old appears to bother some people more than others. I know some senior citizens who will not tell their age! Generally, after 75 when you start getting "special treatments" this makes it all right and the older one gets, the easier it is to "tell". However, consider this comment on aging made by Lucille Ball… "The secret to staying young is to live honestly, eat slowly, and lie about your age." She also knew the secret of laughter! And she never seemed to age.

Actually, there are many benefits to getting older. It gives a freedom one doesn't have in youth. People forgive you for saying things or asking questions you probably shouldn't. You have all those memories you can share or savor yourself. It's easier to be positive and you care less about what others think of you. Not to mention there are loads of discounts that you can get when you reach a "certain age." I like being old. Well, to be completely truthful, I don't think that 75 is old; I don't see myself as old. Probably most people I meet do. I know that this sounds like a contradiction, but…whatever. I'm old and can say what I want!

Of course, age is relative, depending on whom you are with. I had lunch the other day with a friend who is 88 years old and, to her, I was young. The following day I spoke to a college class about the Veterans History Project and probably to them I was old. My best friend forever (BFF in textese…more about that in Chapter Nine.) is only 27 days younger than me and she's not old. So, age is relative. Last summer I met a delightful 95-year-old widow, who was writing her fourth novel. She started writing at age 85 and is published! I immediately went to my local library and checked out her first three novels. I read them straight through! They are really engrossing stories. Her name was Ann Hall Marshall and, unfortunately, she died before she completed her forth novel. She did leave me with some valuable information, in addition to her books. When I asked her how she wrote the books, she said that one must just sit down and do it! I took her advice and here I am.

I found an interesting "pull out" in the Parade Magazine last October 2, 2016. It said to "Pull out and save!" which I did. This article described the seven surprising signs of aging, which I found interesting and will share with you. It didn't talk about gray hair or crow's feet, which I would think of as signs. Let me list them for you; see if you are surprised.

SEVEN SURPRISING SIGNS OF AGING (OR GETTING OLD?)

- Shrinking: Women shrink an average of 1.97 inches from age 30 to 70 years, according to the Baltimore Longitudinal Study of Aging. Most of the shrinkage is normal age-related compression of the padding that separates the vertebrae in our spine. This is different from osteoporosis, which, as you know, is the result of bone loss.

- Drooping Earlobes: "Over the years, sun exposure combined with loss of collagen and elasticity in the skin of the earlobes can cause them to become wrinkled, thin and droopy." says New York City based dermatologist Kally Papantoniou, MD. Years of wearing pierced earrings may also make your lobes more prone to sagging. (If you feel this is a problem, you can see a dermatologist.)

- Sore Feet: It's no wonder that after walking the 3-million-plus steps a year for many years that your feet may hurt. But there is also a condition, called plantar fasciitis, affecting many every year. The most common symptom is pain on the bottom of the foot near the heel in the morning or pain that gets worse after exercise or activity. It is caused by "wear and tear" of the long thin ligament that supports your arch. (Plantar fasciitis can be treated; again… see your physical therapist.)

- Dry Mouth: While dry mouth isn't a direct result of aging, it's a common symptom caused by some medications for age-related conditions, including blood pressure drugs, anti-depressants, and sleep apnea. Dentist Natalie Hastings, San Francisco School of Dentistry, says that if you suffer from dry mouth, you're more prone to cavities, because of low levels of saliva which actually help neutralize acids from foods. She recommends drinking small sips of water or chewing sugar-free gum between meals to help to stimulate saliva production.

- Hairless Legs and Feet: Just as we lose hair on our heads, hair growth on legs may diminish over time. (I don't see the problem here!) However, one cause may be something to worry about. Hair follicles are nourished by blood flow. If your arteries, which deliver oxygen-rich blood to the extremities, clog with plaque, the hair on your legs could fall out. This problem goes beyond poor circulation; it could be connected to heart problems or other medical problems. Dr. Justin Trivax, MD of Beaumont Health's Cardiovascular Performance Clinic in Royal Oak, MI, warns that 60-80 percent of patients with leg artery blockage symptoms have severe blockages in their heart arteries, too.

- Spotted Hands: These are also called "liver spots" but have nothing to do with the health of your liver. They are a sign of sun exposure and common after age 40. They aren't a danger to anything but your vanity.

- Disappearing Eyebrows: If you were "pluck happy" in younger years, you may be paying the price now, with eyebrows that are sparse. The same age-related hormones responsible for hair loss on the head can deplete facial hair. If your brows are suddenly visibly thinner than normal, you can see an endocrinologist since you may have a vitamin deficiency or thyroid condition. It helps if you sleep on your back or on a silk pillowcase to reduce friction. There are other options; you can have your eyebrows tattooed on or purchase an eyebrow pencil.

Well, I will admit to having four of these seven surprising signs. How many can you identify with? I have also heard that your ears never stop growing! And that wasn't even on the list! Maybe the droopy earlobes just make the ears look bigger?

LET'S IMPROVE OUR MEMORY

Okay, now that I have surprised you, I will give you some tips to help you improve your memory. You may not be too surprised with this list, since I have covered most of the tips already:

- Follow a healthy diet
- Keep learning
- Drink alcohol only in moderation
- Get a good night's sleep
- Exercise
- Don't smoke
- Be social
- Manage stress
- Protect your brain from injury
- Improve everyday memory by using your mind

Yes, I have already covered eight of the above. Protecting your brain from injury is a "no-brainer". Of course, it means use the appropriate safety gear during high-speed activities and contact sports. Don't know who is still playing contact sports, but you should wear a good helmet when you ride a bicycle.

There are many specific techniques you can learn to improve your memory. These techniques fall into three general categories: organizational tools, behavioral strategies and memory-enhancing techniques that make new information meaningful and relevant to your, thus making it easier to remember. There are lots of fun things to do on your computer to help you improve your memory also. Take a look.

I am reading a book right now entitled <u>I Can Make You Smarter</u>, by Paul McKenna. It includes two free hypnosis CDs, which may be interesting. Reading is one of the things you can do to improve your memory...and if it makes me smarter too..this book is a winner!

YES GRACEFULLY!

Having said all this, let us age gracefully. Live each day as if it were the last day of your life, because so far, it is. If you choose to dye your hair and erase your wrinkles, do it with joy, and don't be embarrassed about doing so. If you don't so choose, enjoy the gray hair and those wrinkles…you've earned them. Some of the most beautiful faces I've seen were on elderly women in Switzerland and each face was full of wrinkles. Keep your own sense of style but try to keep up with the "fashion trends" for your age. Don't try to wear the current fashions among younger ladies; that is not aging gracefully.

To quote Cindy Joseph, still a model at age 65, "Style comes from knowing yourself, feeling sure about who you are and feeling confident in your choices. One of the many wonderful things about getting older is having a deeper understanding of self." Every stage in life brings something beautiful. Cindy says to allow the character in your face to be your beauty.

FIVE STAGES OF A WOMEN'S LIFE

1. To grow up
2. To fill out
3. To slim down
4. To hold it in
5. To hell with it

(Sorry Cindy...I don't think this is what you had in mind. On the other hand, remember how beneficial it is to laugh.)

LET'S GET PERSONAL ABOUT YOUR BODY

Which brings me to what is called "body image". Why does everyone want to be thin? Well, maybe not everyone. Many of you are satisfied with the shape of your body. I recently heard a discussion about that. Oprah was talking about looking in a mirror at her naked body and thinking that it had served her well for 67 years, and she was going to love it as it is. I have been following her for years, ever since she pulled that little red wagon of "fat" representing the 67 pounds that she had lost, across the stage. She looked awesome in her size 10 jeans (1988). She now calls that her "fattest mistake" because she gained ten pounds in one week when she ate food again. Don't we all love Oprah?

Note: If per slim chance you are a male reading this...you can skip to the next chapter. We ladies need to have some secrets.... and you wouldn't understand what I'm about to talk about anyway.

You have probably engaged in "fat talk," most women do. But did you know that this kind of "personal put-down" can make you depressed, increase your level of stress and whittle down your level of self-confidence? Chances are you may not even realize you're making such statements or that they're self-derogatory. Dr. Shoshana Bennett, a Sonoma, California-based psychologist says,

"You should talk to yourself as you would to a very close friend. Most of us wouldn't dream of uttering to someone we adore the little putdowns we say to ourselves." Remember to be kind to yourself; you are all you've got!

I've decided I'll never get down to my original weight.

I'm okay with that.

After all, 7 pounds 4 ounces is just not realistic!

Well, I hope that made your laugh. I also hope this might convince some of you to stop that "put-down-body" talk and be content in the body you have.

However, there is one complaint that I hear over and over... "jiggly arms!" and "crepey skin." That's two complaints, but they are connected. This is where a bit of extra weight helps "fill out the skin" and may prevent the jiggles and crepeys. Exercises can help some by building up the triceps, the muscles in the back of your arms. Also, it helps to keep the skin moisturized. Look for moisturizers that contain: alpha or beta hydroxy acids, salicylic acid, lactic acid, or glycolic acids. Supposedly, they lubricate and plump skin and decrease the crepey appearance. Retinol topical creams are also recommended. I have to admit that I have not tried any of these suggestions, so let me know if they work. I do know that paddling a kayak once or twice a day does help with toning the upper arms. So do wall push-ups. Oops, that might be an exercise! Anyway, do you think that other people really notice your arms? If you are concerned about this, you can always wear a blouse with sleeves.

I guess another problem we seniors sometimes have is dark circles or puffiness under our eyes. You might recall that these occurred after a night out when you were younger, but if you have them constantly, here's what you might consider. Again, I mention diet. There are foods that are rumored to decrease the "puffy eye bags". Can I call them that? Try eating dark green vegetables like spinach and kale, which have antioxidant lutein; oranges and halos which have vitamin C; red, yellow, orange and purple fruits and vegetables like tomatoes, beets, carrots, sweet potatoes, pumpkins which have lycopene. Also recommended are salmon, tuna, avocado, nuts which contain omega fatty acids; and soy and soy-based products with genistein. (Soy? Did you read what I just wrote about soy above??) Perhaps we should stick to "color" in our diets and the fruits and vegetables which contain good phyto-chemicals. Sometimes too much information is bothersome, but I will continue.

Other studies suggest increasing the amount of collagen in your diet can help reduce the eye puffiness by helping your skin look firmer. Collagen is the most abundant protein in our bodies and is the substance that holds the whole body together. It is especially found in muscles, bones, skin, blood vessels, digestive system and tendons. It's what helps give our skin strength and elasticity along with replacing dead skin cells. Still too much information? Just remember that collagen is very important. We don't want these beloved bodies to fall apart, do we? But where will you find this collagen? Look at the list in the paragraph above....and other sources such as pig's feet, poultry skins and fish. Think I'll stick to fruits and vegetables for my collagen.

To continue with the eye bag suggestions…you can drink more water. Yes! Water is good for you for a number of reasons. Plain, undiluted water. You can also try putting a wet tea bag or cold spoon on your eyes, or anything cold on cotton. I have also heard of putting a slice of cucumber on the eyes for 20-30 minutes. Personally, I think I would rather just eat the cucumbers. Now, if you are really energetic, you could make an eye cream with this recipe.

HOMEMADE EYE CREAM

(Recipe from Dr. Josh Axe, doctor of Natural Medicine, www. help@draxe.com)

> 10 drops of frankincense
> 1-ounce pure aloe vera gel
> 1-ounce unrefined shea butter
> 1-ounce unrefined coconut oil
> ½ teaspoon Vitamin E

Mix all ingredients together. You can gently heat the shea and coconut oil then add the other ingredients. Transfer to a glass jar. Use around the eyes in the a.m. and at night.

No, I haven't tried this either. It does sound interesting. Do you think it would take too long to acquire all the ingredients and where does one buy frankincense? Perhaps it would be fun to research. I do like knowing exactly what products are in the eye cream. Let me know if you try this….and if it works!

❧❧

ARE YOU WAITING FOR MORE BEAUTY TIPS?

Can't give you many "beauty tips" ...but then you are all beautiful in your own way. Life is too short not to think of yourself as beautiful. Beauty is more than skin deep; beauty is on the inside. However, when you look in the mirror, you only see the outside. Cindy Joseph says to allow the character in your face to be your beauty, remember?

You know that diet is a big part of "beauty," which contributes to that healthy look and glowing skin. I also realize that you have had your "beauty routine" for years, and I'm not trying to change that. Here are a few perhaps obscure beauty tips that I can give you:

- When you moisturize your face, don't forget to put the cream on the back of your neck. This is an area we don't see very often, but others do and the back of the neck wrinkles also.
- Use light sandpaper to "sand off" dead skin from heels and feet. It's cheaper than professional remedies and works just as well.
- Coconut oil appears to have a lot of benefits. There are books available that tell you all about them. You can Google "coconut oil" for the titles.
- Get a good eyebrow pencil. With age, eyebrows seem to migrate to the top of your lip and it helps to redefine them. Well, mine migrated. Perhaps yours haven't ...yet. And you can change the arch to fit your mood.

- It will probably be useful to get a good pair of tweezers as well.
- Turn the water to cold at the end of your shower to seal your pores and prevent dirt and bacteria from entering them. Cold water also aids in overall body circulation. Brrrrr!
- This is another widows' suggestion. "Try to stand erect and carry yourself as tall as possible. Try not to shuffle but pick up your feet. However, do be careful and do be watchful not to make quick turns and be thoughtful about each action…being slower is okay." I already put this tip in the section about balance, but it is such a good one, you can read it twice!
- Last tip: It has been said that exercise makes you look better naked. So does wine…your choice!

The below aren't exactly "beauty tips" but you might find them useful. They have been collected from many sources: don't think that I thought them up all myself. Well, I do admit that I have remembered a lot of these from "my past."

- Keep an onion near you at night if you have a stuffy nose. Not sure if I would rather have a stuffy nose or smell an onion all night. My "cure" for a stuffy nose is rubbing good old Vicks around my neck, covered by a piece of flannel or a wool sock.
- Put your hands in ice water and flex them if you have a migraine.
- Press your tongue against the roof of your mouth if you have "brain freeze" from eating ice cream. (Homemade ice cream is worth getting "brain freeze"!)

- Put your tongue against the back of your teeth to prevent a sneeze.
- Pinch yourself if you can't stop laughing. (Now why not just enjoy a good laugh?)
- Scratch your ear if you have a tickle in your throat. (Are you laughing yet?)
- Put deodorant on a mosquito bit to stop the itching. Now, this really does work for me. Remember, I'm still at a place called Wilderness.
- When you stand on one foot to put on your slacks, stand beside a wall but not touching unless you lose your balance. This helps to improve your balance but is not an exercise.
- When putting on a bracelet watch, or a bracelet, put end around wrist and brace wrist against something solid. This will hold bracelet in place until you can fasten it. (You don't need to buy fancy gadget for this purpose.) Or you can tape the end of your bracelet to your wrist, which will hold it until fastened. Personally, I could never find my scotch tape. (Don't forget to remove the tape; you know how forgetful we can be).
- Research shows that the right ear is better at picking up words and speech, while the left ear is better at picking up music and other sounds. "Huh?"
- If you are having trouble falling asleep, blink fast for a minute. Can't try this one right now, I will fall off my bench.
- Another sleep-inducing "technique" is to do this.... Place your tongue against the roof of your mouth while you inhale through your nose for four seconds, hold breath

for seven seconds then blow out through your pursed lips for eight seconds. Repeat cycle four times. For some, this really works!

- If you read a speech before you go to bed, you will remember it better in the morning. This is nice to know if you are still giving speeches.
- If you're feeling sleepy, perhaps when giving this speech, hold your breath as long as you can and then release. Better to do this while your audience is clapping at something you just said.
- When using a public restroom, always check to see if there is toilet paper available before sitting down and "doing your business."
- Safety pins prevent static cling. Place a small safety pin to the inside of your skirt lining or hem of your slacks to prevent them from sticking to your slip and hose. (Hose will make a comeback sometime!) The metal is a good conductor of electricity, so it will divert static away.
- When brushing your teeth, you don't need a full line of toothpaste on your brush, just a "pea- sized" amount will do the job...and your toothpaste will last longer. If you don't believe me, just try it!

☙ ❧

SENIOR SAVINGS

"These 100 Fantastic Senior Discounts Make Us Look Forward to Turning 65"...this was a headline from www.thepennyhoarder.com . (March 20, 2016) This article suggests that you ask for senior discounts, no matter what you are buying. There are too many discounts to list here, but you can go to the website to find if your favorite restaurant has discounts ...or just ask them next time you are eating there. There are discounts on travel, movies, clothing, hotels, recreation venues and many more. However, you must admit your age and ask for a discount.

Well, okay. Here are just a few discounts I found that may pique your interests:

- Regal Cinemas give 35% discounts to seniors
- AMC give 30%. Either way that's enough savings to buy popcorn!
- Walgreens has a "senior's day" once a month (days vary by location) but the discount is 20%
- Kohl's discount is on Wednesdays...over 60 can get a 15% discount
- Goodwill gives a 10-20% discount, day varies by stores
- This one is the most valuable in my opinion. You can get a "life time pass" for America's National Parks. This just went up from $10.00 to $80.00 but it is still a great deal. The pass covers the entrance fee for driver and the passengers, camping and usage fees. Our National Parks are wonderful!

TRAVEL TIPS FOR YOU ON THE GO

Speaking of traveling, I do have a few "travel tips". This is especially helpful if you have trouble remembering things like which gate, departure time and where did I put that boarding pass when traveling by air:

- Take a photo of your passport on your camera or phone; in addition, make a copy or your passport (two copies if you are traveling with a friend and give her a copy to keep). Also have two extra passport photos which will come in handy if for some reason, you lose your passport. Keep your copy and the photos in a separate location, not with your passport.

- Keep travel information organized in a file. Keep telephone numbers, addresses, confirmation number together in one place. I also like to keep a travel journal on each trip; this is a good place to keep the information.

- Put a tag on your carry-on bag that lists flight number, departure time and seat assignment. Then put your ticket in a safe place until needed.

- Note what your travel companion is wearing and keep a recent photo of her. A friend and I usually take a photo of us in the airport prior to departure. This makes a good holiday memory as well.

- If you are over 75 you no longer are required to remove your shoes before you go through security in US airports. (Of course, you have to admit to your age.)

- One last tip that you can use anytime on your digital camera. When I put in a new SM card in my camera, the first photo I take is of my business card, with name, address and phone number, along with a note..." If found please contact for a reward." This is just in case I lose my camera. (Did you hear about the couple who handed their camera to a native who was holding a donkey, for him to take a photo of them holding the donkey....and the native, thinking they wanted to trade, walked away with their camera and left them holding the donkey. Bet the native was counting on the donkey knowing the way home!)

These are all the tips I can come up with at the moment, so will move on to the next chapter. I will leave this one with the following....

Be healthy
Be original
Be patient
Be happy
Be kind
Be You...everyone else is taken

5

Financials:
Money Isn't Funny Anymore

Not that money ever was, but I had to call this chapter something. We're not talking about Monopoly money here. And I really don't have much to say about your personal finances, except to hope that you have enough money to live comfortably. I do realize that some of you will have to continue working or go back to work after your husband dies, because the nest egg never got enough attention. Whichever, you must be aware of your financial situation...your total expenses and your expected income. This will determine your future decisions in many ways.

If your husband had a financial planner, this person is the one to go to for advice. If he didn't and you decide you need one to help you make money decisions, be sure that you work with a certified financial planner. And perhaps it is wise to do a background check or get advice from a relative or friend you trust. In addition, you should pay attention if an investment advisor or promoter uses the following phrases: risk-free, guaranteed earnings, quick profits, the investment is government approved or limited-time offers. This may not be the advisor to go with.

Being military, all our financial business was handled through USAA, a company for military and retired military and their families. USAA stands for United Services Automobile Association, but they handle everything from banking, mortgages, insurance, investments, financial planning and other financial services. I have continued to deal with them for the past ten years and have been very satisfied with their service. The employees address me respectfully as Ms. Redmond, and not Pati, which being old fashioned enough, I appreciate.

USAA, one of the pioneers of direct marketing, conducts most of its business over the internet or telephone. The headquarters is in San Antonio, Texas. The website is www.usaa.com and telephone number is 210-531-8722. USAA is available to all military personnel and their families.

If you are wondering how safe it is to manage financial dealings over the internet, USAA has great security, which includes a "toggle" that one can use to open your personal account. This number, which appears on the toggle, is different each time, and combined with your personal pass code makes good security when you contact USAA.

You can find a lot of financial information on the internet, of course. One of the websites, especially for women, is Women's Institute for a Secure Retirement. (WISER) www.wiserwomen. com . WISER is a nonprofit organization in Washington, DC that is dedicated to the education and advocacy to improve women's long-term financial quality of life. This organization focuses exclusively on women's unique financial challenges.

The America Society on Aging, www.asaging.org is another re-source. It has a blog, called the Age Blog, that has news of interest to us.

FRAUD

Fraud is very real and seniors are particularly vulnerable. In fact, seniors are in danger of being defrauded out of their nest-egg funds or becoming victims of identity theft. According to studies, we start losing mental capacity after age 70 and this gets much worse after 85. Yikes! This doesn't sound good. Also, we seniors apparently have higher levels of trust, losing that "gut feeling", that skepticism, we used to depend on. Actually, a telephone survey showed that one-fifth of Americans over 65 have reported they have been subject to some sort of financial fraud. As Cindy Hounsell, President of the WISER explained, "Older women feel bad they have nothing to leave their relatives, then someone calls up and says, 'You just won!' They all say the same thing…that's why these women fall for it." Generally, you are asked to send a money order or credit card information to "pay the taxes" or for processing and handling… and once that is done…you have been scammed!

There are many ways you can avoid being frauded in investments. Be aware of the "red flags."

- Make sure you are investing with a reliable company. Do research before you invest. Verify licenses and check out the investment. Ask for a prospective or offering circular…

something in writing you can check out.

- Put your phone on the Do Not Call List by calling: 888-382-1222.
- Beware of unsolicited offers and suspicious of high pressure sales; those that state you must act now. Don't make any investment decisions under stress.
- Don't give out personal information until you verify the salesman's credentials.
- Beware of promises of high rates of return and/or "quick profits". If it sounds too good to be true, it probably is.

To check if you are registered with Do Not Call List, call the above number (888-382-1222) and the recording will prompt you how to check if you are still listed. If you are and want to file a complaint about a company that has called you, you should have the name of the company or/and its phone number. Complaints are made at the same number.

Note: However, since telemarketers are now making what is called "robo-calls", there have been so many complaints, that the Federal Trade Commission (FTC) can't keep up. The top violations reported were debt-reductions schemes, vacation and time share offers, warranties and protection plans, and impostors, so keep your eyes…and ears… open for those type of calls and don't engage.

GRANDPARENT SCAM

A scam that has been circulating for a while is aimed at grandparents. The call is from a "grandson" or "granddaughter" who is in trouble, either has been picked up by the police and needs bail money or has lost the passport and money and is stranded in a foreign country. The scammers know the name of the grandchild and have some excuse for not "sounding like them". They are very convincing and ask you to wire money to help. Never fall for this. Call your family and check on the grandchild, but don't wire any money.

Scams and frauds are endless; however, there are agencies that offer help. The Financial Industry Regulatory Authority (FINRA) is the largest independent regulator for all securities firms doing business in the US. FINRA operates the Securities Helpline for Seniors. Telephone number 844-574-3577. The group's website(www.finra.org) provides investment tools, resources and administers the largest dispute resolution forum for investors. FINRA has identified frauds associated with taxes, bogus lottery wins, fake check scams and binary options, (whatever that is.) It reports examples of these frauds on its website as "investor alerts." For example, if you receive a telephone call from IRS, it is fraudulent. The IRS will never contact you by phone; neither will it ask you to wire transfer funds. I have received several of these calls "from the IRS" and I just laugh and hang up.

Note: If you have caller ID and don't recognize the number, you don't have to answer. Scammers have recently been calling from numbers that bear your local area codes, which make you feel safer in answering. This is called "spoofing" or faking a telephone number. You don't have to answer, but if you do and find it is a call from someone you don't want to talk to, just hang up.

If you still have questions or comments about the above, you can Google Elliot Raphaelson. (or email: raphelliot@gmail.com) He wrote an article in the <u>Washington Beacon</u>, January, 2017, entitled "Securities Hotline Protects You from Fraud". He has a lot of information online about scams, consumer disputes and how to protect yourself.

The Federal Trade Commission (FTC) is the nation's consumer protection agency. FTC works to prevent fraudulent, deceptive, and unfair business practices in the market place. Their headquarters is in Washington, DC. Telephone: 1-877-382-4357; TTY: 1-866-653-4261; or website: www.ftc.gov . You can order free publications on topics such as scams, online safety and security, credit and loans and many other topics. Complaints about fraud, scams, phishing, identity theft, unwanted telemarketing, credit or debit issues or other unfair business practices may be submitted to the following: www.ftccomplaintassistant.gov .

Other agencies can provide important information about fraud: the Securities and Exchange Commission, the Consumer Financial Protection Bureau's Office of Investor Education, the North American Securities Administrators Association, and Serving our Seniors.

Unfortunately, most scams are not reported until after they have occurred with the money lost. Since many internet scams are conducted from foreign countries, they are difficult to trace. However, you can contact IC3, the Federal Bureau of Investigation Internet Crime Complaint Center if you suspect a fraud. The website is www.ic3.gov. The mission of the Internet Crime Complaint Center is to provide the public with a reliable and convenient reporting mechanism to submit information to the FBI concerning suspected internet-facilitated criminal activity. Guess you should inquire about an internet agency before you make that invest-ment. Sounds like the safest way.

A Lost Wallet

Of course, there are other ways you can get scammed or have your identity stolen besides via the computer. One is when your wallet is lost or stolen. According to studies of all the cases of ID theft with a known cause, nearly half result from a missing wal-let or purse. This loss occurs three times more often than from data breaches or lonline scams. You can take steps now to prevent problems in advance. You should never carry your Social Security card in your wallet. (Do they still issue that little white and blue card when you get your Social Security number? I misplaced mine years ago, but still remember carrying it in my wallet. Oops!) Neither should you carry a "cheat sheet" of all your pin numbers and passwords. You should have a copy of your Medicare Card in your wallet, but black out the last four digits of the number. You will need to bring the original card for a doctor's appointment.

It is a good idea to make photocopies of the front and back of every card you do keep in your wallet, including your driver's license, insurance cards, credit cards and even your library card. Keep this record at home. In case you do lose your wallet, you will know which cards are lost and have the contact numbers.

If you do lose your wallet or purse, you will need to do the following:

- First determine if it is actually lost or stolen…or just misplaced.

- If you can't find it in all the usual "misplaced places" call your banks and credit card companies to report your loss. (For all credit, debit and ATM cards.) Don't close these accounts, just ask for a new account number. If you carry your checkbook in your lost wallet, you should get a new account number for your checks also. (Yes, you will have to get new checks.)
- Put a fraud alert or credit freeze on your accounts. You will need to call all three credit-reporting agencies. (Names and numbers are listed in the Credit Score section in a few pages.)
- Report your missing driver's license to the DMV. Notify your auto insurer in case the thief makes an accident claim from your policy.
- If your keys are missing also, you will have to change your locks.
- Get a new library card.
- If you lost your military ID card, this will need to be replaced also.
- If your Social Security card was in your wallet inform the Social Security Administration. (See you don't want to carry your SS card in your wallet!)
- If your Medicare card was in your wallet, you will have to report the loss. (This will not be necessary if you carry just a copy of the Medicare card with the last four numbers blacked out.)
- File a report with your local Police Department.

So many things to do to prevent ID theft or loss. Perhaps this will convince you to clean out your wallet and carry only those necessary items. That will cut down on the work which is necessary if your wallet is ever missing.

AND MORE SCAMS

More? Yes! Scam artists are just about anywhere, online, on your phone and even at your doorstep. Be aware of someone who knocks on your door or calls you and says they are doing work for a neighbor, and wonders if you want your "dead" tree cut down, or your roof repaired, or driveway resurfaced. Of course, they offer to give you a good deal, because "they are in the neighborhood". Some of these offers may be legitimate. But beware, many aren't and you will have paid out cash…they generally want cash…and work may not be done or done poorly. There are also scams connected with your cable connection and your utilities. If you do succumb to "such a good deal", you might want to take a photo of the individual and of his vehicle license plate, just in case you are not satisfied with the work or do get scammed. As a general rule, don't let a stranger into your home without proper identification.

Actually, I never let a stranger into my home. I have storm doors on all my doors and they all have a dead-bolt lock. If someone rings my doorbell, I talk through that locked door or I don't open the door. You don't have to open the door if you don't recognize the person. I always keep my doors locked. Unfortunately, times and people have changed. I grew up in a small town in Ohio where doors were rarely locked. Even if locked, the key was placed under the flower pot or above the transom…and available. We were never robbed. No doubt this has changed now, even in small-town America.

CHIP CREDIT CARD

Banks and credit card companies are in the process of issuing customers new "chip" cards. This will make your credit and bank cards safer, because of the new technology; they're almost impossible to counterfeit. (At least at this time.) However, there could be a scam involved even here. Con artists are impersonating card issuers and sending emails requesting personal and financial information before "they issue your new chip card." Keep in mind that no credit card company will email or call you to verify personal info it already has on file before mailing a new card. If you are unsure, call the number on the back of your card and ask if they are trying to contact you. Your new chip card may require a four-digit pin number.

So, "rule of thumb" …(do you still remember that saying?) … is to see through the phone and online scammers and assume that any stranger who calls or emails you "to make you rich" is a liar and just wants your money! This includes calls about "Free Federal grants", from the IRS, the FBI, or messages on Facebook or a dating site by someone claiming to be a lonely US soldier, sailor, airman or Marine., who eventually asks you for money. Don't be gullible!

CREDIT SCORE

Do you know what your credit score is? Credit scores range from 300-850. Scores above 680 are good, while scores below 620 may indicate credit problems. It is a good idea to check your credit report at least once a year. There are three credit bureaus and you are allowed a free credit report from each one annually. They are:

Equifax, Experian, and TransUnion. (Equifax at 800-525-6285, Experian at 888-397-3742, TransUnion at 800-680-7289)

It is advisable not to use a cellphone or tablet when attempting to get your credit score. Although the websites are secure, the wireless network that you are using to get to the site may not be. If you use your mobile device, your personal information, including your Social Security number, may be at risk. It is recommended that you use your regular desk computer, which is equipped with a fire wall and security system, to get your credit reports. (So, don't use the computers at your local library!) Actually, once a year you can go to www.annualcreditreport.com and get all three credit reports for free.

Guess I should get one of my daughters to help me write about computers and what they can do. They grew up with computers and even my three-year-old grandson can "operate" his mom's phone and his "mini-computer". This is the computer age and the technology is wonderful…if you understand it. There are computer classes for seniors available and it is advisable to take a course if you are really curious about what computers can do. However, if you get "stuck" you can always ask a grandchild…or any child…for help. Actually, you don't even have to know how computers work, just how do get them to do what you want them to. It may be intimidating at first, but once you learn the basics, it's not so hard to operate a computer. I will explain further about the wonderful "tech age" in Chapter Nine.

But I digress again…back to financial matters.

SOCIAL SECURITY NUMBER

Be careful to whom you give your Social Security number. Only a few organizations have a legal right to your number; they are your employer, banks and lenders, investment funds, the IRS, and government funded programs. You can say no when asked by others. You are not even required to provide this number on forms at the doctor's office. However, if you are on Medicare, this is presently the way the provider can uniquely identify you. This will change in 2018 when Medicare numbers are changed to numbers that do not use your Social Security number. Many states have already done this on driver's licenses. This should help cut down on identity theft. In many instances you are asked for the last four digits of your Social Security number, and this, apparently, has been fairly safe. However, new information I just received stated that the last four digits are truly random and unique. The first five numbers represent when and where you card was issued. Scammers can get those numbers by knowing your birth date and hometown. If you give your "last four" freely, they will have the whole Social Security number!

MEDICARE

Your Social Security Office will help you get established with Medicare when you register to start receiving Social Security. If you are confused about which plan to sign up for, you can go to the Medicare website for resources to help you find a plan. The official US government site for Medicare is www.Medicare.gov. A non-government site powered by eHealth is www.Medicare.com (note this ends in "com", not "gov") and it has information, but it is not official. Don't forget Medicare coverage does not offer us "free insurance"; we pay for it each month via the amount deducted from our Social Security check.

Medicare does not cover any medical service abroad, except in rare circumstances along the Canadian and Mexican borders. Keep this in mind when you are traveling outside of the United States. You can always purchase travel insurance if you want medical coverage during your trip.

Tip: Another tip to remember; you can have a free "wellness" doctor visit once a year covered by Medicare. You must ask for this by name. If you ask for a "physical" it will be a more comprehensive exam and may not be covered completely by Medicare. However, in many cases, your secondary insurance may cover the expense.

IRA's

Great! You have invested in IRA's through your working years and do have a nest egg. Congratulations! There is one thing that you should know about IRA's. Many couples may have dropped into a lower tax rate after retirement. But after age 70 ½ you must start taking Required Minimal Distributions (RMD) annually from tax-deferred accounts like a 401(k) or traditional IRA. These distributions, along with other income, can push you into a higher tax bracket again. As a couple, your income of $75,900 puts you in the 15% bracket. As a widow filing single, income over $37,950 moves you from the 15% bracket to a higher tax bracket. The "extra" income from the RMD can cause an increase in income, thus an increase in taxes. Your financial advisor can help you with this. This information may change with the 2018 tax revisions.

INCOME TAX

If you want to save money in doing your taxes, you might want to consider the free tax help for seniors. Many Senior Centers offer this service. The IRS has the Volunteer Income Tax Assistance (VITA) program which offers free tax help to people who make $54,000 or less and Tax Counseling for the Elderly (TCE) for those age 60 or older. If you are connected to the military, the Judge Advocate General (JAG) also offers free tax preparation on military bases.

KIDS AND YOUR MONEY

Perhaps you may wonder what you should tell your children about your money. Financial planners say it's important to have "the talk" with your children. Jane Bryant Quinn, a personal finance expert and author of <u>Making the Most of Your Money Now</u>, (which is an excellent personal finance book), advises that you might not want to tell your children exactly what you're worth, in case your assets get depleted later in life. This way they won't plan on an inheritance they might not get. Quinn says even though you choose not to tell then your exact worth, they probably should know whether or not you have enough income and savings to live. You might want to explain some provision in your will now, so that after your death they will understand why you made those decisions. Even if you don't feel that you can talk about that now, at least leave a letter with your will explaining your reasoning. Also tell them who will be the executor of your will or have the power of attorney. They should hear this from you. This may keep the peace in your family after your death and avoid hurt feelings among the siblings.

As you get older, it becomes more important to talk to the children, in case you become ill or incapacitated and need help with your finances. You should be organized; have a list of your assets, information about the location of your will and important papers such as your birth certificate, Social Security papers, and a list of passwords for all your devices, and remember to keep it updated. They will need to know about banks accounts, investments, and other important financial information. Also, if you are on medication, make a list of all you are taking, your physicians and their contact numbers. This list is good for you to have anyway, especially if you are seeing numerous physicians and they are all prescribing medications. If you have a pet, list your veterinarian and the number and any medications your pet might be on. You can put all this information in a folder and instruct your children where it is located. It is also where you can list items that you want to be distributed to individuals after your death. These things may not be in your will.

It is suggested that you prepare an advanced directive, which consists of two parts; a power of attorney and a living will. Execute a durable power of attorney so someone can make financial decisions on your behalf if you're unable. I have already discussed this in Chapter Two.

"GRAB AND GO" BOOK

Mary M. Benzinger, Senior Attorney at the Pentagon Army and Air Force Legal Assistance Office, suggests you have a "Grab and Go" book with all this important information listed. You can use any notebook or one of those pretty little journals you find in most stores. Put it someplace safe, but let your family know the location. This is also a good idea just in case your home catches fire and you need to exit quickly. Just grab the book and go!

BACK TO YOUR CHILDREN AND YOUR MONEY

Have you heard that this present generation...or perhaps your children's generation, I'm onto my grands generation by now... whatever, this generation is the first one that will not have higher "standard of living" than you, (their parents) have had? Does this mean a higher quality of life or just "more toys"? I'm not sure what or why, but this does appear to be the general case. Your children may be constantly "short of cash". Thus, your predicament ...how much do you offer them and on what terms? You probably know that you can give a child, their spouse, and each grandchild a total of $14,000 every year without involving gift-taxes for them. That's a lot of money to give away, but that is the law. In some cases, if not all, this is enabling. If your child knows that s/he can count on you to "bail them out" s/he may never learn to budget...or to live the life style their income is providing. Of course, I am sure that you want the best for your children and grandchildren. So, if you are financially secure and can "help" them financially, it is your decision. I do know that childcare expenses are outrageous for working parents and in many cases, costs more than their monthly mortgage. It is a conundrum.

Note: I have read that this tax-free gift limit increases to $15,000 in 2018!

CLEARING CLUTTER IN YOUR DWELLING AND DEBT

Nationally syndicated columnist Michelle Singletary, who writes the "The Color of Money" in the <u>Washington Post</u>, advocates that you should declutter you dwelling and your debt. This does seem like a good idea for everyone to follow. I am guilty of office clutter myself. You probably all know that one should keep tax records for seven years after filing, but do you know that you should keep your tax returns indefinitely? She also writes that you should keep a copy of the will for up to three years after the estate is settled. If you want more information about what records to keep you can Google this and ask specifically about the document in question or just ask "what records to keep and what to discard".

It is recommended that you keep a copy of the funeral programs for family history. I have been doing this because I am a member of the Daughters of the American Revolution (DAR) and know how important it is to keep records of family history. Obituaries also have a lot of information which may be useful in the future. (Of course, this is not decluttering, but these items won't take up much room.)

I missed her article on decluttering debt but can guess that she suggests trying to get rid of it. She was talking about credit card debt. Website: www.michelle.singletary@washpost.com

SHREDDER

If your husband didn't have a shredder, you may want to buy one. With the very real threat of identity theft, you need to take steps to protect your identity. It is important to get rid of any paperwork that has personal information. All these unnecessary papers should be shredded, not just thrown away in your trash. Sometimes banks or other organizations have "shredding events", special times you can take a box of papers to be shredded, or you can take unwanted paperwork to a professional shredder company. You will probably have a lot of this when you start to clean out your husband's files. In my community, we have a professional shredder whose business is called "Shred, White and Blue", which being patriotic, I think is a fun name.

The following is a list of papers you should shred when no longer useful.

- Address labels from junk mail and magazines
- ATM receipts
- Bank statements
- Canceled and voided checks
- Credit and charge card bills, carbon copies, summaries, and receipts
- Credit reports and histories
- Employee pay stubs
- Expired credit and ID cards including driver's licenses, any ID's, employee badges, medical insurance cards.
- Expired passport and visas
- Legal documents
- Insurance documents
- Investment, stock and property transactions
- Luggage tags
- Medical and dental records
- Papers with a Social Security number

- Pre-approved credit card applications
- Receipts with checking account numbers
- Report cards
- Resumes or curriculum vitae
- Signatures found on letters, contracts, letters
- Tax forms
- Transcripts
- Travel itineraries
- Used airplane tickets
- Utility bills (telephone, gas, electric, water, cable, Internet)

Note: Many of the above items should be kept for various lengths of time, generally one to seven years. Records such as home purchases/sales, warranties, legal records, insurance retirement and pension records, and investment trade confirmations should be kept permanently. However, you can discard credit card receipts or bank deposit/withdrawal slips once reconciled with your monthly statements.

If you decide you would like to keep anything on the list, be sure to file it in a safe place. Personally, I love to keep my outdated passports, so I can look at them and remember the places I've been. I guess the point is, that if you are discarding anything that is on the list, it should be shredded rather than just tossed in the trash.

Pet Savings

I really enjoy my Irish Setter, Rojo, and am glad I have her as my companion. She was the last puppy my husband and I picked out together, so she is approaching her "senior years" also. We are growing old together. Of course, veterinary bills are costly, but there are ways to save. One way to save is to make sure you do the preventive care, such as heart worm medicine, flea and tick protection. These precautions may save costly infections caused by these parasites. These medicines for the heart and fleas have a wide range of prices. You can shop around and check the internet for pet web sites. Your veterinarian may match the cheaper price or even write you a prescription so you can order the cheaper online medications. Your local pharmacy can also supply some medications that your pet may require.

Note: Be sure your purchase prescription products online that are made by a reputable US pharmaceutical company.

There may also be alternatives to expensive procedures suggested by your vet. An example is teeth cleaning. A lot of breeds have problems with tarter build up that can require expensive dental cleaning under anesthesia. When Rojo's vet suggested this cleaning technique, I asked if there was an alternate method of cleaning her teeth. He suggested I try an oral care water additive which I added to her drinking water daily. It actually works! (Fresh Breath by Tropiclean). Along with dental chews, it helps take the tarter off her teeth.

Dog's ears can sometimes be a problem; Rojo has had an infection in her left year only for years and, although I have seen four different vets, it has not been cured. One of the veterinarians suggested she might have allergies and I should try "gluten free" dog food. I shopped around for the "gluten free" dog food and found that there are many varieties that are cheaper, and comparable to the one recommended. (Apparently, after many tests, it was determined that she didn't have an allergy to grains, which often is the case. However, I never thought it was an allergy. After all, the infection was only in one ear; why not both if it was an allergy?) I have learned to deal with her problem.

Sorry but I can't give any suggestions about cats or birds or any other pets you might have. I think there are "dog people" which both my husband and I were, and then there are "cat people". Guess you will just have to talk to your cat loving friends for information.

GIVE YOURSELF A VALENTINE

Before I leave this chapter, I would like to pass on information gleaned from my Frederick News Post business section (February 14, 2017). It's a valentine to yourself. The title of the article, written by Liz Weston, reads: "It's OK to spend money on yourself—really". She explains that although people generally spend too much, there are some who are too frugal, and I think she might be talking about us widows. "Spend" may not be a good word for one who is frugal, but planning helps you know what is important in the long run and what to spend money on now. She suggests that you have a budget and the "just for fun" spending will come out of the income that's not already allocated. As stated previously, memories are better than dreams, and what better way to treat yourself than to take that trip to "wherever" that you have always longed to visit. "Experiences tend to give us more lasting pleasure than things" Weston writes, "but the right purchases also can be an investment." Perhaps you should talk things over with your financial planner. If you would feel better about spending money on yourself without worry of over-spending and wrecking your budget, you can set up a special bank account dedicated to this trip or purchase. That way you will have the money up front so you can enjoy your trip, knowing that it is paid for.

Now, to digress again…Sometimes the female swan honors me with her presence. She comes up on the bank and sits down beside me for a while. Rojo greets her by ignoring her. Of course, "Lovely" (swan) is my friend…I give her corn every day. (Note: never feed bread to birds. Yes, they like it and eat it, but it's not in their diet normally. Corn sometimes is.) Lovely is visiting me now, and a Blue Heron just landed beside me on the lake. I call herons the "stealth" birds because they move so quietly and have such patience just to stand there until the fish arrives. Also, nearby on the lake is a family of Canada Geese and two Mallard duck families. Isn't this an awesome place?

It has been said that money is evil, but this is not exactly true.…

"For the love of money is the root of all evil"
…I Timothy 6:10

6

It Doesn't Take Long to Make Half a Bed

This chapter is about your taking care of your home. Can you tell? Yes, I know. You are wondering where I got all these crazy chapter titles. I told you that I'm not related to Heloise, and so you know I didn't get them from her. But I do think of this every time I make my bed. I find it a lot easier to just make one side, not having to walk around the bed and straighten all the pillows and covers. My husband and I had an unwritten rule which just made sense …whoever was the last one up made the bed. Therefore, since he was an early riser and I liked to sleep in back then, I generally ended up making the bed. Now I only have to make half the bed because I never sleep on "his" side of the bed. I wonder how many of you do this? Actually, it saves laundry, too. I just flip the sheets and sleep on the clean side instead of changing the whole sheet and I also trade pillowcases. I do realize that you have established cleaning routines after all these years, but perhaps you will learn something new.

MATTRESS QUANDARY

An interesting question is how often the mattress should be replaced. The "rule of thumb" is that you need a new mattress every eight year. However, I think that was drummed up by the mattress companies, because our mattress is still very comfortable and it was purchased several years before my husband died. Jeff Frank, owner of Ecommerce website specializing in unique furniture products, says, "This simple question has been hotly debated within the mattress industry for the past 50 years. The answer changes periodically." So perhaps my reasoning is correct? Wouldn't you think that one would need to take into consideration who was using the mattress, their weight, size, and the quality of the mattress. If you are not getting a good night's sleep, you might sleep better on a new mattress. Remember, years ago mattresses were stuffed with straw. I bet they were "changed" more frequently than very eight years.

Just another note about mattresses; the newer ones usually don't have to be routinely flipped over, as we did with older ones. They just have to be rotated occasionally; meaning, just spin them so that the foot of the mattress goes to the head of the bed. This is quite easy to do; I can manage it myself. Flipping a mattress is a lot harder. It is also a good idea to vacuum your mattress once in a while, which will remove dust, and lint but hopefully, no bed bugs.

HOUSE CLEANING

Now, I realize that you have been cleaning your homes for years, and if you are lucky enough to have a regular cleaning lady, you can just skip this chapter on household hints. However, there may be some obscure tips that you have never heard of, so perhaps you should at least skim it. As I said…I'm not related to Heloise or even to that wacky old broad that gives you ideas on the internet. (She does make me laugh!)

Note of caution: one of the widows commented, "I would like to find a good cleaning lady. It is hard to reach these ceiling fans, change light bulbs and get into corners while vacuuming. Why don't I call someone?? Because one drawback here in Florida is a fact that several people have been robbed, cheated and deserted by cleaners who were thought to be trustworthy! In this area, it is prevalent and has happened to many of my friends. So, it is an element of trust with me at the moment." I am adding her comments here, because it is another way we seniors can be frauded. Remember, we are too trusting. Guess you should get a reference from a friend before hiring a cleaning lady or go with a bonded agency.

GERMIEST SPOTS IN YOUR HOME

You may guess the toilet, but actually the number one dirtiest spot is the bathroom sink! Yes, sinks are often dirtier than the toilet seat. If you close the toilet lid before flushing, this will save many germs from escaping into the bathroom. My husband always cleaned the sink after he shaved, so I sort of forget about cleaning it, thinking that since I don't shave, it won't get as dirty. Not true! A good way to clean and disinfect at the same time is to spray on an anti-bacterial formula and let it sit for about five minutes before wiping. Goodbye by germs!

Another germy area is you telephone…do you still have a landline phone? I need mine to call my cell when I can't remember where I left it. Also, germs love doorknobs and handles as well as switch plates, so disinfect them often.

One more "germy note". The germiest places in a restaurant are the menu and the seats. If you place your order first, then go to the restroom and wash your hands, or use that cute little hand sanitizer you carry in your purse, before you eat, you can eliminate some germs. But keep your hands off the seat!

Digital devices are often forgotten and I wouldn't think of this if my daughter hadn't told me about canned air. Yes, I did say canned air and I'm not talking about the local windbag. You can actually buy this, probably at Walmart, and use it to clean the crumbs and dust off your keyboards. Or you can unplug the keyboard and use a dampened lint-free microfiber cloth over the keys and into the grooves. Do not use anything that is dripping wet on electronics. I learned that the hard way when I spilled my coffee on my new laptop. I killed the mother board, whatever that is. It didn't make my husband too happy. Cell phones are also breeding grounds for bacteria. You can use the little lint-free wipes that you clean your glasses with, or the microfiber cloth. If you are really concerned, you might consider ordering product called PhoneSoap 2.0, which is a UV light that sanitizes the phone while charging it. Website is www.phonesoap.com .

OTHER HOUSEHOLD TIPS

- You probably all know about using baking soda to keep your refrigerator smelling better, but did you know that instead of discarding it after a while, use the old soda to clean your drains. Pour it down the drain and add a vinegar chaser. Let it sit and bubble for a while before rinsing. Don't you love to recycle?

- Talking about recycling, in Maryland you can get $50.00 for your old refrigerators. The electric company's recycling program will pick up your working fridge or freezer and "responsibly recycle it". You can check with your electric company to see if they have the same deal. As you know, old refrigerators are "energy hogs."

- A lot of household cleaners can be made from items in your pantry. Vinegar is probably the number one choice for cleaning a lot of items. Also useful is dishwashing liquid, as well as baking soda. (more about that below.) Heloise has all kinds of recipes that you can get from her website www.Helosie@goodhousekeeping .

- Test the seal around your refrigerator by placing a dollar bill in the door and closing it. If the bill pulls out easily, you probably need a new seal. Heck, you can use a $5.00 bill and get the same results. Seals can be purchased from store where you obtained your refrigerator or from your brands company, and you may be able to replace them yourself. However, it would be easier for your handyman to do it.

- "Vampire" electronics consume electricity even when turned off. This means electronics and other plug-in household appliances and devices that continue to use electricity even when they are turned "off". Unplugging electronics can save you as much as 10% of your electricity bill. You can use power strips, which will cut electricity to off devices.

- Replace or clean the filter in your furnace and air conditioner regularly. This will save money on your heating or cooling bills.

- Coffee filters are good for many purposes besides holding the coffee grounds. I am talking about the round filters, not the triangular ones. Place one in your bag of lettuce to keep it fresher longer. (a paper towel also works, if you are not a coffee drinker. Not a coffee drinker? How do you survive the mornings?) Use one to serve snacks to the grandchildren. I used coffee filters to keep my knees from further burning one day when I had sat in the sun too long. Use your imagination, they don't cost very much.

- Don't forget to clean out the dryer lint trap after every use. These appliances start thousands of home fires every year.

- Throw out all those Teflon pans that were made before 2012. They contain chemicals that have been found to increase the risk of cancers. Stainless steel and cast iron are better choices for cookware.

- Peroxide has many other uses as well, besides cleaning cuts and scrapes. You can use it to sanitize tooth brushes, as a produce wash to keep fruits and vegetables fresh longer, and to disinfect cuttings boards. More ideas for its use at www.using-hydrogen-peroxide.com

- Do you know that bell peppers have "genders"? Four bumps (lobes) on the bottom indicates a female which are full of seeds but sweeter to eat raw. The male pepper has three bumps and is better for cooking. Who knew and where did this information come from??? Further research said that this was "false news" and it didn't matter how many bumps the peppers had...but I think it is a "fun fact" that may or may not be true. Bet you look at the bottom of the next pepper you buy.

- Another really useful product is Bounce, the fabric softener I often use. There are multiple uses for Bounce, beside in the dryer. It is rumored that the US Postal Service told letter carriers to put a sheet of Bounce in their uniform pockets to keep yellow-jackets away and it is also rumored to repel mice and mosquitoes. (I know that one maintenance man who works a Wilderness, carries Bounce in his pocket. He showed me and swore it keep all those unwanted critters away!) It also eliminates static electricity and freshen air in your car as well as deodorize your sneakers. This one I have never tried…run a threaded needle through a sheet of Bounce before beginning to sew and it prevents thread from tangling. Maybe you should check with your letter carrier first, but I have Bounce on my shopping list. If you are curious about more ideas, the website is www.Bounce.com .

- Clutter…we all have it. You can use clear shoe boxes, which are available in many stores and inexpensive to store many small items like batteries, small toys, art and office supplies, photos, small toiletries…get the idea? This will help you keep organized.

- This is not a new tip, but some of you may not have heard about using tooth paste to clean jewelry. Just rub a bit into your rings, necklaces and earrings with a soft brush…or your finger. Rinse will with warm water. A note of caution; don't use this with delicate items or pearls.

- If you have not already done so, become familiar with a few basic tools. Know how to us a hammer…hold it by the grip, not close to the head. The claw end is helpful for pulling out nails. There are two main types of screw drivers, straight and Phelps. Check the head of the screw for a straight line or an "x" which requires the Phelps. Plyers, tape measure and Duct tape…you can Google "basic tools for home" for more. Before you rush out to buy a hammer, look for your husband's tool box. You will probably find all you need there. One of the things I was told was to not sell my husband's tools to some "bargain hunter". You can use a lot of them yourself. Whenever I need to so a "minor job" like hanging a photo or fixing something, the tool I need is always in my husband's toolbox.

- To sharpen a dull knife without a knife sharpener, rub it on the bottom of a red clay pot.
- For a natural pest control, plant marigolds in your garden. They also deter the deer who love to chomp on your flowers.
- This tip won't do you much good unless you build fires at your campground. Save toilet and towel paper rolls, stuff them with dryer lint and use them as "fire starters." Talk about recycling!
- Make sure you don't leave your house keys in the door when you come in with an armful of things. Not only will you allow a thief easy entry, you will also go crazy looking all over your house for your keys!

LOVELY GLASS TOP STOVES

Many of you may have the newer glass top stove. Last time we purchased a stove, I figured it was the last time, so we did get one.

I really enjoy it, not that I do much cooking, but I do find it difficult to clean, so I did some research just in case you have similar problems with your "last" stove.

I found this information from as many sources as there are stoves. I picked six of the best. Some took more elbow grease than necessary. Needless to say, first you have to make sure your stovetop is completely cool.

1. Scraping Method: put a liberal amount of liquid cleaner to the burnt-on stains. Use an old plastic credit card, or any similar card to scrape. I use those "trial" plastic credit cards that often come in the mail but are not activated. Actually, a salesman told me about this method when I asked to buy a glass stove top scraper. He said it worked just as well as the one he was selling. You can also scrape with a razor blade, but be careful since it could scratch the finish.

2. Towel Method: this method uses good old vinegar and baking soda. Wipe the surface off with vinegar and sprinkle a generous amount of baking soda. Drop a towel in hot water and wring out. Lay towel on stove top for 15 minutes. This will loosen the stuff on the stove top so you can scrub away the gunk with an abrasive topped sponge. (Why not use a credit card?) Don't use a metal abrasive pad which may scratch the surface. This sounds rather messy and too involved for me.

3. Vinegar and Baking Soda Method: sprinkle baking soda and then spray with vinegar. Let sit for 15 minutes and wipe away with a wet rag. Guess the stove above had more gunk? (But you don't get your towel dirty!)

4. Silicone Spatula Method: I'm not sure what this is and don't
    have one, but if you do, first rub stains with it in a circular
    motion to loosen the gunk. Mix 4 tablespoons of Baking Soda
    and 1 Tablespoon of vinegar to make a paste. Place it over the
    stains for a few minutes, probably 15, then scrub stain off
    with a microfiber cloth. Wipe down with a wet cloth.

5. Ammonia and Alcohol Method: Mix a solution of 1-part am-
    monia and 10-parts water with 3 ounces rubbing alcohol.
    Spray on glass top and let sit. Wipe down. Well, at least it's
    not using Baking Soda and Vinegar.

6. Dish Soap Method: and finally, swirl some liquid dish soap
    on top and then sprinkle Baking Soda over the entire surface.
    Splash a little bit of hydrogen peroxide and mix solution to-
    gether with your finger. Use elbow grease and a scrubber to
    clean. Wipe down with a wet rag. Didn't say anything about
    letting it sit for 15 minutes. Maybe this is the method to use
    if you are in a hurry to get that gunk off the glass top?

Okay, so take your choice of these methods. I guess you have
surmised that I use the first method, so probably I should have
just told you this is how you do it. However, it is nice to have
choices, so I gave you all six methods. You are going to have a lot
of choices to make now, endless choices, some big, some small.
So, you can practice by making the choice about how you are going to clean your new stove top.

However, if you skip all the above and just buy the specialty cleaner, here are a few tips for that. You still must wait until the stove
burners are cool first. Avoid cleaners with ammonia or abrasive

materials which could scratch or stain the cook top. The best ones I have found are made by Weimen or Cerama Brite (which has a cleaning pads combo kit.)

Note: You should never use a cast iron skillet or other heavy cookware that can also scratch the surface of your stove. And avoid dragging a pot on the stove. Be careful when cooking with sugar and don't spill it on the stove top...or clean up spills quickly, lest they discolor the stove top. Lastly, and I have done this, don't place hot bake wear on the stove top...even with hot pads. Place your cakes and cookies right out of the oven on a hot pad or dry towel on your counter. Now we both know!

GIVE YOUR APPLIANCES SOME TLC

They require some tender loving care routinely. Wondering who has thought about cleaning the dishwasher or washing machine... when not doing a load? Distilled white vinegar will take care of both these tasks. For the dishwasher, place a cup of vinegar on the top rack and run a full cycle with hot water. You can also deodorize the dishwasher by sprinkling baking soda on the bottom and running it again with hot water. Afterwards, leave the door open for a few hours to air out. When you wash with hot water, your washing machine is cleaned well, but it's a good idea to run it empty with a cup of vinegar to sanitize the basin every month. You probably already know to leave the door open between washings if you have a front-loading washer. This will prevent mildew from developing.

Have you ever had your Mr. Coffee machine stop working? The problem could be hard water minerals that have built up and shut it down. The solution? Vinegar to the rescue! Fill the reservoir with vinegar and let it run a cycle. You can use an empty filter to keep it neater. It is suggested to let it run through for half a cycle and turn it off for about 30 minutes, then turn it on and let it continue brewing. I would probably forget to do this and then have vinegar-coffee next morning. Be sure to run two more brewing cycles with clear water to remove the vinegar taste.

Cleaning the refrigerator is a BIG job. You have to remove everything and clean the interior with a solution of baking soda and warm water. (1 tablespoon mixed with 1 quart of water.) It's a good idea to do this routinely, then you can toss all the forgotten foods that are hiding in the back. You probably won't be able to move the refrigerator away from the wall to vacuum, but perhaps you have a handy man who can wrestle it. When you put the foods back, remember that the top shelf is not the coldest area and so put milk and other items that require a consistent temperature on the middle shelves. The bottom shelf is the coldest, so store meat there. Who knew? I got these ideas from an article written by Elizabeth Mayhew that appeared in the <u>Washington Post</u>, January 5, 2017. She also suggested that you clean the garbage disposal by running through a cutup lemon, a couple of tablespoons of salt and a few ice cubes.

The microwave is easy. Use several slices of lemon or again, white vinegar in a cup of water and turn on high for about three minutes. Let it steam up the glass window. Open the door and wipe down the interior with a clean cloth…or paper towels. Actually, you should clean the microwave anytime you have heated liquids that have splattered, before using it again so they get "baked on."

Have you ever heard that you can tell if someone is a good house-keeper by the cleanliness of her microwave? I haven't either, but don't you think that is a good analogy?

A Record of What You Own

Have you ever thought of taking a home inventory? It's an excellent way to expedite the insurance claims process after theft, damage or loss. Actually, a good and quick way is to make a video of each room and store it on a CD. However, if you still like pen and paper, you can get ideas from Google again if you ask for a home inventory list. Before you scoff and say to yourself, "I can remember what I own!", try this test. Sit in your kitchen and make a list of everything in your living room or dining room. Then check to see how many items you have missed.

You should record every major item in each room, with a description of each. If you can remember the purchase date and price is also useful. Major appliances electronics have serial numbers, generally located on the back or bottom. (Get the handy man to note the number of your refrigerator when he has it pulled out.) Also, if you have the receipts from an item, keep them with the list. To back up your written inventory, photograph each wall of each room with closet or cabinet doors open. On the back of each photo…you will have to make "hard copies" of the photos… write the date, the general location and contents shown. Or you can take photos on your cell phone and store them in the "cloud." Your written list should be stored somewhere in a safe place away from your home…just in case your house burns down or is blown away by a hurricane. (Sorry, did this thought cause an increase in stress? See Chapter Three again.)

HOME MAINTENANCE

If you can't stop that leaky faucet, you can get directions from …yep… you can just Google "how to fix a leaky faucet" and get good step by step information. Of course, you can also get your handy man to repair it and not worry about it yourself. It would be another challenge, however. Wouldn't your husband be proud of you if he knew that you fixed that leaky faucet yourself?

HIDDEN HEALTH RISK

I recently met Pat Lerouk, who is a home inspector in Frederick, MD county, and he gave me some valuable information I am going to share with you. Have you heard of radon gas? It is a naturally occurring radioactive gas that results from the decay of uranium found in trace amounts in soil, rock and water. Radon is the main source of our exposure to all radiation, and while outdoors is not a threat, radon gas can enter into our homes and accumulate to dangerous levels. Because we spend so much time indoors, exposure to such levels of radon over a long period of time can pose a serious health risk.

According to the National Safety Council, radon is estimated to cause 21,000 deaths in the US every year. It has been determined that radon is second only to smoking as a leading cause of lung cancer. You cannot see, smell or taste radon. Any home can have a radon problem and the only way to know is to test. Mr. Lerouk suggested that before you sell your home, you should have it tested for radon, and you should determine that any home you buy be tested as well. If your home has never been tested for radon, he suggested you contact a reputable Environmental Protection Agency or State listed radon mitigation contractor for a proposal.

HOME MAINTENANCE CHECKLIST

Mr. Lerouk also discussed the care and regular maintenance that a home requires. This is something that I hadn't really thought about before, but I have had to get a new hot water heater, several new appliances, and the house painted in these past ten years. He suggested a routine home maintenance inspection which will evaluate all major systems of the home, including plumbing, heating, electrical, air-conditioning and structure. He also gave me the following checklist that can be incorporated into regular maintenance program to keep your house in great shape. Now don't get discouraged, because the list is long.

- Change the backup batteries in smoke detectors and carbon-monoxide alarms and dust their covers.
- Change furnace and air conditioner filters.
- Check fire extinguishers.
- Clean out gutters and downspouts.
- Call the chimney sweep.
- Check all window seals.
- Check the attic and basement for leaks.
- Check for damage to your roof.
- Check the water heater for leaks or rust.
- Check the kitchen exhaust hood and air filter.
- Clean the clothes dryer exhaust duct and damper, and the space under the dryer.
- Check the nightlights at the top and bottom of all stairways.
- Check the exterior siding.
- Check all window and door locks.

- Check your home for water leaks.
- Test your emergency generator.
- Confirm that firewood is stored at least 20 feet away from your home.
- Familiarize yourself with the gas main valve and other appliance valves.
- Test all CFCI (ground-fault circuit interrupter) receptacles/outlets.
- Renew your emergency escape plan.
- Make sure your house number is visible for the street for first responders to see.
- Replace all extension cords that have become brittle, worn or damaged.
- Contact the professional home inspector annually to perform your home maintenance inspection.

Actually, most of the items on the above list are really just common sense things that your husband probably did regularly. I did remember about changing the batteries in the smoke and carbon-monoxide alarms periodically.

But we're not done yet with the care and maintenance.

CARE OF DRIVEWAYS

Who thinks about driveways? If you are a widow who is still driving, the who is you! Look at your driveway checking for cracks or bumps, scrapes from last year's plowing…plowing, that's another thing to consider. Know that contractors are not all the same; be sure you hire one who is bonded or licensed. You can always ask your neighbor who he uses to have his driveway resurfaced or sealed. Sealing is usually the first option and much less expensive than resurfacing is. Sealing lasts for two to three years; resurfacing lasts longer. I guess it depends on how bad your driveway is whether you have it sealed or resurfaced.

Cleaning snow off your driveway. Shoveling is good exercise, if you are in good enough shape. I have found that if the snow is light, either that it will soon melt and doesn't need to be shoveled, or if a bit deeper I will shovel it. I push the snow to the side of the drive instead of lifting the shovel. It's easy to do if the snow is light and fluffy. However, it the snow is deep, it is advisable to have it plowed. Women can have a heart attack when shoveling snow just as men can! Again, neighbors are helpful or you can hire a service to plow. I love the snow and don't really mind shoveling. I still love to make snow angels as well. Remember how to do that?

SAFETY IN YOUR HOME

This must be addressed because you are now living alone; this means personal safety as well as making your home safe and secure. Several widows commented that after their husband died, they didn't feel safe being alone. Perhaps this is a good time to get a dog. However, if that is not a consideration, there are many things you can do to make your home safer for you and give you more protection.

Are you aware of the ads demonstrating the "alert" buttons that you can activate if you fall? Two that I have seen advertised are Life Alert, (1-800-404-0735) and Medical Alert, (1-800-369-6695). They advertise that they will bring immediate help in any emergency. You will want to do your own research before purchasing such a system. I have never actually investigated either system; I just see their ads in various senior publications.

I do have a funny story about a patient I saw when I was doing home care PT. She wore one of those alert necklaces and one day put in a load of laundry. When she leaned over to put the clothes in, somehow, she activated her alarm. I forgot to tell you, she lived in the downstairs apartment of her daughter's home. The fireman came and when they knocked on the front door, they didn't get a response, so they used their axes to knock down the door! In the meantime, she was happily in her basement apartment, until one of the firemen happened to walk around and saw her. Don't know who bought the new front door, but the point I'm making is be sure to tell the "responders" if you live in a basement apartment!

There's a lot I can tell you about safety, but I will try to limit it, as not to lose your attention. I just saw an interesting ad in a catalogue by First Street. It tells about "safety hip protectors" which help "disperse the impact of a hard fall"! They come with an anatomically shaped hip-protecting pad with shock absorption and may work, protecting your hips from a fracture if you fall. I have no idea if they work. It is advertised as "the next generation of hip protectors"! If you are interested, you can call 1-800-704-1210 or go to www.FirstStreetOnline.com and request their catalog.

It is a good idea to adapt your home, even if you don't need to make changes now. Do an annual safety review so you can make necessary updates if your home needs change. Stairs, bathroom and kitchens can present hazards for older people.

Many falls occur in the bathroom, as you get into or out the bath tub. Be sure to use a non-slip mat in your bathtub or shower.

Of course, safety grab bars will help stabilize you, but there is another option if you can afford it financially...the Walk-in Tub. I do know of a senior who had one...and loved it. If you want more information about these tubs, you can contact 1-800-806-2676 for your free information kit and DVD, and their senior discount. You can also obtain a tub seat that fits into your tub for a less expensive option.

Lighting is very important. Do have good lighting so you can see where you are going? All your stairs should be well lit and have a railing...which you hold when navigating them. Remember what I promised my daughter? Also, don't "store" stuff on your stairs. If you want a clever and safe idea, have a basket at the top...or bottom...of your stairs to carry items you mean to take down...or up.

OTHER SAFETY TIPS

- Don't use stepstools. Keep the items you need within easy reach.
- Okay, if you use a stepstool, it is safer to use one that has an extension you can hold onto when you climb. I "borrowed" the one my daughter had and never gave it back. Thanks, Erin.
- Remove small rugs that can cause you to trip.
- Secure electrical cords and phone cords as well.
- Think ahead about how you would get help if you have an emergency or fall. Keep emergency numbers near each phone...or in your contact list on your phone. Carry your cell phone in your pocket (gee, then it would never be lost!)...or consider investing in some type of personal alarm system, as discussed above.

- Keep fresh batteries in your smoke and natural gas detectors. The Firefighter Safety Research Institute suggests testing all detectors once a month. Mine will emit a horrible noise when the batteries are weak, so it's better to check periodically than be awoken by that racket!
- Instead of carrying a heavy pot of water between the sink and stove, use a pitcher to fill the pot on the stove.
- Use night lights to guide you from your bed to the bathroom and don't leave anything in the path that you could trip over en route.
- Replace all door and faucet handles with lever- style handles which are much easier to use.
- If you don't have deadbolt locks on your doors, it is a good idea to have them installed. Adding another sturdy lock to all exterior doors is perhaps one of the best safety improvements you can make to keep your home safe.

OUTDOOR SAFETY

My husband had the electric company install a pole light in the driveway, which lights my path from my car into my front door. I pay a small fee each monthly on my electric bill for this service. It the light goes out, the electric company repairs it, as they did when a bird built a nest in it a few years ago. Or you can use solar light fixtures to light the pathways of your home. They are relatively inexpensive and powered by the sun.

Landscaping is also important. You can use proper landscaping to deter burglars by planting roses or any sort of prickly plant underneath windows that could be possible entry points to your home. Avoid having large shrubs that someone could hide behind near the windows. Keep the lawn mowed, especially when you are on vacation; uncut grass is an invitation to the burglar. (Yes, my neighbor is cutting my grass while I am gone.)

HOLIDAY HOME SAFETY

With all the excitement and festivity of the holiday season, it can be easy to overlook the potential hazards. Here are some tips you can use to help ensure your safety during this joyous time:

- Lock all doors and windows when leaving the house...even for a short time. For an extended leave, have a neighbor get your mail and install an automatic timer for indoor and outdoor lights. You can also have your mail on hold at the post office.
- Mount your tree on a sturdy base, at least three feet away from any heat vents, radiators and fireplaces and make sure your artificial tree is fire-retardant.
- Replace strings of lights that area frayed or broken. Turn off all tree lights before you go to bed or leave the house.
- Some holiday plants such as mistletoe or holly berries can pose risks to small children and pets. Keep them out of reach.
- Never leave candles unattended or near flammable materials.
- Open the flue before lighting a fire and use a screen when the fire is burning.
- Have a safe and happy holiday.

Live life going forward;
understand life by looking back.

7

Ladies Start your Engines

"John Dear" ...Yes, that's what I call my ride-on John Deere lawn mower...the one my husband said I would never be able to control. "He" is a dear ...when "it" starts. And I have been mowing my acre and a quarter for the past ten years. I know that most of you don't have a "Dear John" mower to cut your grass, but I am going to show you that you can learn new things; perhaps even things that you never thought you could do. I have learned all sorts of things about "John" ... what sort of gas he likes, how to pry off the little battery caps and pour in distilled water, how to prime it, and what prayers to say when he won't start the first time. Actually, I have to admit, my next-door neighbor taught me all these things. Well, not the prayers. He also keeps "John" in shape by changing the oil...a task I will never learn to do...and changing the blades when the old ones needs sharpening. I know where to take them to get them sharpened and buy the oil filters. John Deere stores are really "men's stores", but they are really nice to me. And it's really wonderful to have helpful neighbors. I have found that you can always ask a man if you want to know how to do "man-kind" of things. I take notes, so I don't forget the instructions.

I have heard that oil in the lawn mower should be changed every ten hours, which for me would mean about every fourth mow. That may be a good idea, but I must admit, I generally only have "John's" oil changed every season. My neighbor's name is John also, and he gives me advise that I don't always take.

My husband also had a manual push lawn mower for the tight places "John" couldn't go. It is old and dusty...and starts every time I pull the cord. This always amazes me. It takes regular gasoline also. I know it should take better care of it as well, and I do check the oil and put gas in it. There are probably things I should do in addition, but I haven't checked what is needed. It starts... if it's not broke, don't fix it. However, if you have a push mower, you should probably ask a man what is necessary (is that sexist?) ...or read the manual that came with it. My husband would have the manual in his file under "maintenance."

Tip: At the gas station, when you put gasoline in one of those red gas storage cans, be sure to put the can on the ground before you put the gas in it. Don't leave it in the back of your vehicle while you put the gas in it and also don't leave it in your car very long after you fill it or your car will smell like gas. (See the reason for this precaution in the gasoline section below.) Probably a lot of those cans your husband had are five-gallon cans. Now that makes a heavy can to lift in and out of your car and hold while you pour gas into your mower. I usually only put three gallons of gas in the can and it is much easier to handle. Of course, there are smaller storage cans you can get, but that means you have to fill them more often.

Mowing grass is really rather fun...especially when you are

finished and you can sit in your swing and look at the results. My husband always said to mow in different patterns every time, which gives a better-looking cut. And boy, do I! There are a lot of trees in my yard, so it's never a straight cut back and forth. I like to do diagonal's the best, and mow circles around the trees. If you are a mower, be sure to wear safety goggles or at least sun glasses to protect your eyes. I generally wear a hat also, to keep the sun off my face and just in case I hit a branch, the hat helps to protect my face. Did I mention that it's dirty work to mow? Especially when it hasn't rained for a while and there is a lot of dust. Sometimes I look like the masked man with a bandana tied around my nose, sun glasses and a sun hat. (Remember, we don't care what others think of us!)

Okay, moving on. I know you all don't have a yard to mow or perhaps you have a yard man who mows for you.

ABOUT AUTOMOBILES

Next issue: do you know how to drive? This may be a silly question. However, maybe you did drive years ago, but since your husband did all the driving, you haven't driven for a while. You may need a refresher course. Call your local DMV or MVA to see if there is a course in your area. These courses sometimes are mandatory if one gets too many tickets, and if you do take one, you may get a break in your auto insurance.

In any case, you will need transportation. You can depend on friends only so long. There are driving schools, of course, but with practice you will probably re-learn to drive quickly, and soon feel confident driving again. Perhaps you have a grandchild or friend who can "practice" with you. Do I need to mention, you should have good vision, and a driver's license? Depending on when you got your last driver's license, it may be good for an extended number of years but check the expiration date. And if your doctor or children have suggested you are too old to drive, ignore this paragraph.

GASOLINE

If you are driving again, you will need to get gas. There are no longer cute young men who used to run out to your car to pump the gas; you have to do it yourself. I really miss those days. You might need to learn how to pump gas. There are generally three grades of gas, and your car will require a specific level, so you need to know this. Generally, you can use your credit card and pay at the pump. Some stations require cash, but that's where the cheapest priced gas is.

I was going to say you need to know how to check your oil, but this has changed also, with newer cars. We used to change oil after 3,000 miles, but today's synthetic oils are good for around 7,000 miles, or even up to 10,000 miles. This all depends on your vehicle and the type of oil it uses, so you need to know that basic information. If you do a lot of "stop and go" driving you might need to change your oil more frequently than you would if you do more long-distance driving.

You may have noticed that the prices vary from gas station to gas station. I have a favorite gas station where the price is the lowest in town; it also requires cash only. That's how they keep the price down. If you are on a budget and want to check for the best gas prices in your area, you can download apps that allow you to check without running around looking at the signs. "Gas Finder", "Gas Buddy" and "Fuel Finder" are just a few to consider. If you don't know how to download an app…again…just ask your grandchild or any teenager. In addition, many supermarkets allow you to earn gas savings while doing your grocery shopping. Big box stores, which require membership, also have cheaper gas and if you have their credit card, you will get "cash back" for your gas purchases. There are lots of ways to save money on gas!

Rumors started circulating in 1999 about how cell phones can cause a fire in the presence of gasoline fumes. However, the FCC states there is no evidence that these reports are true. While it may be "theoretically possible for a spark from a cell phone battery to ignite gas vapor", the FCC concludes the potential threat is remote. Even so, all major oil companies have, as a preventive measure, banned cell phone use at gas pumps. This may soon change with modern technology. At some gas stations there are even mobile pay apps for filling up at the pump. (No, I have never used them. But no doubt, they will be more common by the time this book is in print.) Soon, you will be able to use your cell phone while you are "gassing up" and won't have to ignore a sign that says "Turn off your phones while refueling".

There is a safety tip that you might not be aware of…that fires can be started by "static electricity" at the gas pumps! Bob Renkes, the retired executive vice president of Petroleum Equipment Institute (PEI), stated you should NEVER get back into your vehicle while filling it with gas. The static from your body can cause a fire. (This is more likely to occur in the winter.) He said that if you absolutely have to get in your vehicle while the gas is pumping, make sure you get out, close the door touching the metal, before you pull the gas nozzle out of your gas tank. This way the static from your body will be discharged before you ever remove the nozzle. If a fire does start, never take the gas nozzle out of your car. That is the surest way to turn a bad situation into a tragedy. Everyone who has been hurt, injured or has been killed, has pulled that nozzle out.

A total of 78 percent of these fires happen to women, says static electricity expert Steve Fowler. Why? Because they women tend to get back into their cars more often than men. If you have passengers in your car when you stop for gas, make sure everyone unbuckles their seat belts while you are filling up. If there is a fire, they will be able to escape more quickly…and it will be easier for you to rescue your grandchild. Better still, never get gas when you have little children in your car. As discussed above, never fill portable containers in or on a vehicle. Instead, put them on the ground. Like a person, a container can also become statically charged. If the earth's not there to absorb the voltage, the can itself may spark.

Here are the "three rules for safe refueling":

1. Turn off engine
2. Don't smoke
3. Don't re-enter your vehicle during fueling

TIRES

If you get your tires rotated when you have your oil changes… which is a good idea so they will wear more evenly. The mechanic will check the air pressure in each tire, so you won't have to worry about that either. It is a good idea to know how to check the air in your tires with that cute little air pressure gauge. There is a label on your driver's door that tells you the amount of air pressure necessary and it is also listed on the tires. Tire pressure can go down in the winter as the air gets colder. Driving with under-inflated tires will damage them and then you may have to buy new tires. This is generally a fairly costly purchase. And since I am talking about tires, the way to check the amount of tread on tires, is to stick a penny between the groves. If you can see Abe's head, it's probably time for new tires. (Be sure to turn the penny with Abe's head going in).

Your mechanic will generally tell you when your tires need to be re-aligned. If they are not aligned properly it is more difficult to handle because the vehicle tends to pull toward one side of the road rather than traveling in a straight line. A good way for you to tell if your vehicle is aligned is to let go of the steering wheel while driving at highway speeds and if your vehicle pulls one way or another and needs an alignment. (You shouldn't try this when you are in traffic. Guess that is a "duh"!)

I was thinking about putting in instructions for how to change a flat tire. However, that is a pretty physical thing to do. This is a great reason to have roadside assist. Just call the number and let the mechanic do it for you. (See Safety on the Road below.) In case you do have a flat tire while you are driving, slowly guide your car to a safe area, as far away from the traffic as you can get. Switch on your hazard lights, put your car in park and set the parking break. Then call your road side assist.

Note: A spare tire is a temporary fix. Get to a repair shop as soon as you can to have your tire repaired or get a new tire.

TUNE-UPS

You will have to keep your engine tuned, so talk to your mechanic about that. Your husband probably had a mechanic, so you can use him, or ask a male friend where he would suggest you take your car. If your car doesn't "tell" you when, there should be a little book in the glove department that will give you a schedule. If you have repairs done on your vehicle, get the estimate in writing. My last repair was over a hundred dollars above the "estimate". Men know these things. I wish I had thanked my husband for taking such good care of my cars.

FIXD

I just discovered that there is a new automotive diagnostic device called the "Fixd" that easily attaches to your auto. It instantly tells you if there is a problem with your car! It informs you if it is an emergency, something that should be fixed soon, or that you don't have to worry about it. Now I have not purchased this, and it sounds expensive you say? However, it has very good reviews from the people who has one, and it costs only $59.00! (Also, there are sales which drops the price to $39.00 if you buy two, and you get a third one free.) You will save that much the first time you go to some dishonest mechanic where you could get charged for something completely unnecessary. Unfortunately, all mechanics are not honest. If you had this device, you could check and see if your mechanic is.

SAFETY ON THE ROAD

You might want to consider getting a "road side assist" plan, in case your car breaks down or you get a flat tire when you are on the road. There are a lot of plans available, through AAA or your insurance company. I use Sam's Roadside Assist (not Sam's Warehouse) and it has worked very well for me. Of course, you would rather not be inconvenience with a break down or flat, and it is nice to know what to do if this occurs. This plan usually includes towing also if you have a serious problem and your car won't start, or if you have an accident.

When driving try to avoid sudden starts and stops, which will save you money on fuel and future maintenance. Also, don't run out for just a single errand, if you can help it. Combine your errands so you don't make so many trips. Clean your car of "junk" and bring in that large bag of dog food immediately …or those golf clubs. Extra weight in the trunk requires more gas. Of course, you should keep the normal safety items in your trunk, like a flashlight, an ice scraper and brush…and a spare tire. In addition, battery jumping cables, a shovel, extra batteries, a blanket, snack foods, water and extra warm clothes may be useful if you live "up north" where there's a chance you could get stuck in the snow. This probably won't happen to me: I live in Maryland and we rarely get those lovely deep snowfalls…and if we do, I certainly don't drive. However, maybe you will get stranded. It's good advice to stay in your car, start your engine occasionally to run the heater, but don't keep your car running. That's when you will need that blanket and extra mittens…and snack foods and water.

WINTER DRIVING TIPS

Since I told you what to keep in your trunk in case you get stuck in the snow, maybe it's a good time to give you some driving tips so you won't get stuck when the weather is bad:

- Increase visibility: remove all snow and ice from your car, including windows, lights, mirrors, hood, roof and trunk. I have found that a long-handled brush works well for this. If you turn on your engine heater first, that will help melt the ice. Also, it you spray a mixture of alcohol and water on your windshield prior to the snow, that will keep a lot of snow from sticking. (one third water, two thirds rubbing alcohol mixed well in a spray bottle.) Some drivers also pull the windshield wipers out from the windshield... they stick up and stay put...when snow is forecast. Then the blades don't get stuck to the windshield. However, when I tried this, a branch fell on one of my wipers and broke it. So now I leave them in place.
- Slow down: if your car has antilock brakes, gently press to slow down. If you don't have antilock brakes, you must gently pump the brakes at a rapid pace when attempting to stop on ice and snow. In other words, don't just slam on the brakes, because that will initiate a slide.
- Control the skid: Don't panic! Take your foot off the brake and accelerator, steering into the direction of the skid to gain traction. Slowly accelerate.
- Use caution on bridges and overpasses; these areas freeze first.
- Never use cruise control in snowy or icy conditions. (Or when it is raining.)

- Drive in cleared lanes and don't pass snowplows or salt trucks.
- Stay home and sit in front of a roaring fire. Do you really need to go out?

DEAD BATTERY? YOU CAN HANDLE IT

If you turn the key and your engine doesn't start your may have a dead battery. Don't worry…you can "jump your car" when the battery is "dead". Jumper cables have red and black clips on both ends the cord. Your battery has two large terminals, one positive, one negative. You will need another vehicle to "jump" your battery. The drivers of these cars are called "Good Samaritans". Both cars should be in neutral or park with the ignition shut off and the brakes on. Attach one of the red clips to the red (positive) terminal of your battery and the other red clip to the red terminal of the other battery. (the positive terminal may have a + or pos on it and is bigger than the negative terminal.) Attach one of the black clips to the negative terminal on the other battery. Attach the last black clip to an unpainted metal surface on your car that isn't the battery. Start the rescue car and let the engine run for a few minutes. Then try to start your vehicle. If it won't start, check to be sure you have the cables properly connected. The clips are rather hard to secure and one may have fallen off. Have the Good Samaritan run the engine for a while longer and then try to start your car again. If you do get your car to start, remove the cables in reverse order for safety. It is also advised to wear gloves and safety goggles when you attempt to jump the battery. If your car won't start, your battery may be beyond rescue. This is when the road side assist becomes very useful.

Tip: When attaching the cables, remember this little rhyme and it makes things easier…. "Red from the dead, to red on the good. Black from the good to under the hood."

I know it's a bit scary to have to mess with car batteries. If you can't understand the above, you can Google "jumping batteries" and see how the cables are attached. It really isn't as difficult as it sounds but has to be done correctly. In case you can't find the jumping cables you husband had, you can purchase them at any auto supply store, like Pep Boys or even Walmart's for a better price. They are not very expensive.

LEARN TO USE A GPS

One of the things I can recommend is if you use a GPS (Global Positioning System) when you drive to an unknown location, don't put in your actual home address. It is suggested to put the address of your local police department or at least a gas station. After all, when you are in your local area, you know how to get home. I'll give you an example why you shouldn't put in your home address. You are at your grandson's baseball game when someone steals your car. They plug in your GPS and they can go to your home address and steal everything they can carry from your home. They know you won't be home for a while or even miss your auto until the game is over.

It amazes me that the little car you see on your GPS screen depicts your car traveling down the road. Isn't modern technology marvelous? And wouldn't the potential car thieves be surprised when your GPS took them right to the local Police Station???

SHOULD YOU BE DRIVING?

I would be remiss in this chapter unless I talked more about "listen to your doctor or daughter" in regard to when to discontinuing driving. Of course, age alone is not the limiting factor to whether you should drive or not, but age-related physical changes can impact your driving skills. Glaucoma or cataracts may comprise your vision. Arthritis may make it difficult to turn your head, grasp the steering wheel, or put your foot on the brake quickly enough. If you have an annual eye exam to check for any vision changes and make sure your glasses prescription is up to date if you do need glasses to see distance. If you stay current on the "rules of the road", you should be fine. But, if you find yourself driving at 30 miles per hour on an interstate, which causes all the other vehicles to pass you, perhaps you should revaluate your driving skills. If you are fearful of driving at the speed limit this may be when you should stop driving. Also, to quote another elderly widow, "No driving at night should be a rule."

DANGEROUS SITUATIONS FOR OLDER DRIVERS

The Motor Vehicles Administration provides a "Resource Guide for Aging Drivers" to help drivers and their families deal with issues that come with getting older. This list of potential problems is from Maryland Motor Vehicle Administration:

- Turning left at an intersection with a stop sign
- Turning left at an intersection with a green light without a left-turn arrow
- Turning right at a yield sign to merge with faster-moving traffic
- Merging from a highway ramp with a yield sign
- Changing lanes on road with four or more lanes

It's OK if You Don't Drive

If you don't drive and don't have friends to depend on, there are "new" ways to get transported. Most towns have what is called Uber or Lyft drivers who come when called...again you will need an app on your phone to contact them. I haven't used this service, but it is considered controlled and safe. You will have credit with the company, so no money is involved during the ride and it is rumored that you don't even have to tip to driver. Of course, there are taxies, buses and airport vans available in most areas. And if you are adventuresome, you could probably find a college student or young person who would like to make some extra money driving a sweet old widow around. Shades of "Driving Miss Daisy"?

Last tips: If your car is driven under 5,000 miles a year, ask your insurer for a low-mileage discount. You may be able to save money on your insurance. In addition, if you admit to being "over 70", you may not have to do the biennial DMV "Vehicle Emissions Inspection" that is required in most states.

And for the widow of a veteran, you should qualify for a "military discount of $500" when you buy a new car. (I recently got a Ruby Red Ford Escape AND the military discount!) You will need to show the dealer your military ID, your husband's DD214, and his death certificate. (If he tells you that you don't qualify, ask him to read the fine print.)

I've never been able to explain my car trouble to a mechanic without using sound effects.

8

Do You Think
It's a Couples' World?

"I was supposed to spend the rest of my life with you.

And then I realized that you spent the rest of your life with me.

I smile because I know you loved me till the day you went away.

And will keep loving me until the day we're together again."

I don't know who wrote this, but I smile when I read it, after I wipe away the tears. Having faith, I know this is true; but I am alone now, in a couples' world. Renowned author, Mary Higgins Clark married her husband Warren in 1949. They were married for 14 years when he died in 1964. She writes, "I missed being married. I missed the companionship, the closeness, the friendship that is the essence of a good marriage. The world goes two by two." She says this so much better than I could; it is a couples' world. Anyone who has lost a spouse, can tell you this. You wake up to another day, say good morning to the world, and then you remember...half of you is not there and never will be again. We have already talked about grief, that it is such a personal issue, and how each widow handles her grief differently. Widowhood is something you have to grow into by yourself, and unfortunately, this is sometimes made more difficult because of the "couples thing".

Some of my widow friends complained that their friends, who are couples, ignored them after the husband died and wondered why this happens. There are several reasons why friends drop you when your spouse dies. When a friend or contemporary dies, it makes you think of your own mortality. Your spouse's absence may be a constant reminder. Perhaps they think a widow is emotionally needy so they don't want to be involved with her. However, in some cases, the wife is afraid of the "competition." Yes, I'm talking about you...a single lady. I know it sounds trite but be observant when you are talking to a couple. Who does most of the talking? Is he talking to and looking at you and ignoring his wife? Are you flirting with the husband with all your attention on him, or including his wife in the conservation? Are you an attractive widow who has read the chapter about keeping up appearances and being aware of the fashion trends for your age? This may surprise you to know that some wives will find your new single status a "threat" to her husband and that may limit your friendship with them. Indeed, the wife may be jealous of you. I don't think jealously has an age limit. Perhaps she is afraid you are out to "steal" her husband! On the other hand, this couple may just be inconsiderate, and you don't need to continue this relationship anyway. It is not a true friendship. You can find new friends, married, widowed and single and can enjoy being with them.

Another reason is that friends may not invite you is because they are afraid you will feel like a "third wheel." Perhaps you should tell these friends that you would love to be included and please do invite you. I no longer feel like the third wheel when friends invite me to go out, and I accept the invitation. Another widow wrote, "I prefer not to date, and no longer feel like a third wheel if married friends do ask me to join them for some social event, but I am pretty adamant, though I hope kind, about paying my own way!" Of course, many events don't matter whether you have a spouse along or not.

I do miss talking to a man. Men have such interesting views on things and some are such excellent conversationalists. My husband and I used to have lovely conversations, even if they were just about the day. It is different talking to a man. They think differently than my female friends or I do… as different as Mars is to Venus. This is something that I doubt a married woman even thinks about. Girlfriends, I am not flirting with your husband; I am just enjoying our conservation! And along that line, remember men know a lot about things we women don't know… or perhaps even care to know…but necessity calls, now that we are widows. If you want to know something your husband would have known, guess what? Ask another man!

Note: Just don't make a habit of asking the same man questions all the time; this could make his wife jealous or suspicious of your intent.

HEARING WEDDING BELLS AGAIN?

Have you ever thought about remarriage? Are you looking for a man to spend your "golden years" together? Or do you feel that no one can replace your husband? Perhaps, like some widows, you haven't found a male whose company you prefer to you own? When my single BFF from grade school and I went to our 50th class reunion, I jokingly offered that she could have the first pick from the now nine "bachelors" in our high school class. Her reply was, "Pati, if we didn't want them when we graduated 50 years ago, we won't want them now!" (Sorry guys, guess you would know who I am talking about, but the chance of you reading a book about widows is pretty slim.)

Widowers remarry more than widows, possibly because men are more dependent on their "day to day" care. How else do widows and widowers differ? It is said that women morn; men replace. Men are less burdened by guilt, they are the beneficiary of limitless "fix-ups" and winner of the role of "the extra man" at dinner parties. Perhaps they just have better coping mechanisms? (And widowers have more choices than widows do! The ratio of widows to widowers is 4:1!)

However, statistics do show that remarriage is on the rise for Americans 55 and older. Doctor Meredith Ruch, a clinical sociologist in Princeton, NJ, noted that older widows have a real hesitation about remarrying. "These women, especially those who have had successful marriages and careers, are whole unto themselves. They don't have anything to prove," says Dr. Ruch. One of the widows I spoke to about this commented that widowers were often just looking for someone to take care of them in their old age! Actually, she said, "American men are looking for nurses with purses."

Many widows who remain single recognize their ability to do so rests on two essential points; financial independence and the ability and wiliness to live a life as an individual rather than one of a pair. For you widows who have become very independent, a man would "cramp your style"! Just think of what you would be obligated to do with a husband:

- Cook regular meals again
- Consider someone else's schedule or wishes …or wants
- Have a new family of relatives, children, grandchildren, to consider
- Let someone else decide what to do, to eat, when, et cetera
- Have another tooth brush in your bathroom
- Have another person around all the time (who may get in your way)
- Have a lot more chores to do daily
- Including more laundry
- Do men still need to have their shirts ironed?
- Have competition controlling the thermostat
- Loose your former husband's Social Security and/or military benefits

Enough…guess you get the idea how I feel! However, if you are fortunate enough to meet someone who "turns your head" and you fall in love again, congratulations! I hope you will have a good life together and make many new memories. Many assume that a widow who manages to move ahead and be happy again probably didn't love her partner much in the first place. However, studies show there's no connection between the closeness of the marriage and the depth and duration of mourning. Those with healthy, happy relationships were well positioned to go on with healthy lives…which may or may not include a new husband.

(Nevertheless, I am going to stick with the memories I have already made. So, again I say, "Friends, please do keep in mind that if I talk to your husband, I am not trying to take him away from you. Just think how nice it is to have a conservation with a man.")

∽◦◦⌒

Silver and Gold

And now I will segue into friendship…couples or not. Friendships are especially important to you now, as a widow. Do keep old friendships close. They are a joy to have. "Pick up your phone and call old friends on the spur of the moment or on a holiday, just to let them know you're thinking of them. Don't forget to send cards and notes. We all know they are appreciated." This same widow also suggested that you keep a supply of small gifts and treats to share with those who take the time to visit or help you in some way. What a thoughtful idea!

As I have said previously, do not isolate yourself or become a recluse hiding away by yourself and refusing to build a new life. It is what it is. Your husband is not coming back. The next chapter of your life is yours to do what you want. As you grow into widowhood, you can actually be selfish and do exactly what you want. Hopefully you have done your grieving, but if you are still in the process, friends can help you through it. They will hold your hand, listen to you talk, remember events and laugh with you. Initially, this is ideal, but don't depend on their support for too long. This was an issue discussed by several of the widows in my "control group." Some suggested you attend support groups or a grief class. They found it helpful to not be isolated in their grief. One widow said she didn't want to hear other's sad stories; she wanted to be up lifted. I was on this page when I attended a Grief Share gathering at my church. I was more depressed listening to the other widow's stories of their loss. I only attended one meeting.

Just a word or two here to a friend, who might know a widow. Call her occasionally, invite her to lunch or send her a card. It is nice to be remembered. I recall that a widow told me, right after my husband died, "When someone offers to help you, accept their help. Because after the first year, people generally forget that you are a widow who could use some help." I have found this to be true. People do forget. They expect you to "get over it" and go on with your life. Recognize that as much as you wish to have support, you will have to forge your own way through your heart ache. However, since we are still talking about friendship, you can offer the new widow support better than your "still married" friends. You have been through the loss and the grief process. In doing this, it will help you to grow into the role as well.

New friends are silver, old friends are gold!

9

ETC ...Electronics + Technology = Confusion

Before I get into this chapter, I would like to say "Happy 4th of July"! Today, as I write this, we are celebrating America's freedom and independence. Bushels of thanks to our American Revolutionary ancestors and the Declaration of Independence authors and signers who made this day possible. I hope we can all remember that the motto of our country is "In God We Trust" and, when the "Star -Spangled Banner" is played, we will continue to stand with our hand on our hearts as we sing those words penned by Francis Scott Key in 1814. He was inspired by the British bombing of Ft. McHenry during the War of 1812. He, by the way, was a native Marylander and is buried in my town of Frederick, MD. I just found out on the internet, of course, that "E Pluribus Unum" (Out of many, one) considered a de facto motto of the United States until 1956 was never codified by law. The modern motto of the United States, "In God We Trust," was adopted by Congress and signed by President Dwight D. Eisenhower in 1956. In 2011, it was reaffirmed as our national motto by the House of Representatives.

Okay, enough history. Remember the above; it may be on a cross word puzzle you are doing someday. As you can see, our widows book is coming along. I should be able to finish writing by Labor Day...perhaps.

Let the fireworks begin!

ELECTRONICS + TECHNOLOGY CAUSES CONFUSION

Well some of you may be technical wizards, but probably the rest of us are confused with the recent developments in technology. What happened to telephones, books, newspapers, and writing letters? Technology! I recall years ago when we heard that in the future we could see a person who was calling us, we laughed and said, "Not on your life!" But it has happened, and we have also had men land on the moon. There are also plans for some rich people to take a trip to Mars!

And here they are...I-phones, Skype, I-pads, Kindles, laptops... and all the social networks. We can email, text, tweet, Facebook, blog, chat and probably communicate other ways I haven't even heard of. If you do get involved, you may be surprised what old friends you will meet again. And you can catch up with your grandchildren on Facebook. Many find that it is easier to text a message than to call someone. They say if you learn how to text you can increase your communication with all of your family. Actually, it is true. A text you can read anytime, and don't have to stop what you are doing to pick up the phone! And isn't it grand to be able to see your grandchildren via Skype? Do you know what I am talking about, or have I confused you again? Well, I will try to explain some things; however, I must warn you, I still get very confused myself. In fact, this laptop computer is a mystery to me still. Last week I inadvertently hit some key I didn't mean to, and this whole book went into "editing mode" which caused little black dots to appear between every word! Having no idea what to do about it and was afraid I would delete the whole book if I tried to do anything. Yesterday I was rescued by a computer tech friend who showed me the way to "get out" of there.

So, where do I start? It is estimated that the majority of seniors do have a computer (PC) or access to one. Don't let these terms intimidate you. It is advisable to take a computer course offered at community colleges or through Senior Learning Centers. Many community colleges offer an Institute for Learning in Retirement (ILR) for those 55 and older. Keep in mind that the computer keeps evolving…it may be a ploy by the computer companies to make you buy an updated one. Do you think? Did you know that as of April, 2017, Microsoft stopped security updates, assisted support or online technical content updates for Windows Vista customers? If you continue to use Windows Vista now that support has ended, your computer will still work, but it might become more vulnerable to security risks and viruses. Do you recall the most recent scams that required all those companies to pay ransom to have their computers "unlocked and released"? This is because they were all outdated, no longer protected and easily broken into. So it pays to keep current and to have a good security system, such as Norton or Trend Micro Security.

DEVICES

Computer: Also called a PC or personal computer.

Laptops: They are just small computers, so if you can use a computer you can use a laptop. You might not appreciate the rather small key board and the finger pad, but if this is the case, you can add a keyboard and a mouse, and it turns into a regular computer.

TABLETS

Kindle: A Kindle is a line of Android-powdered portable e-book readers' devices developed by Amazon that enable users to shop for, download and read electronic versions of books, newspapers, magazines, websites, blogs and more. The Kindle DX features larger screen than the original Kindle.

I don't own a Kindle, preferring to read a hardcopy book. However, many of my friends do own them and love them. I understand they are great to use when your travel. It saves room in your luggage if you don't have to bring books you plan to read. However, they run on batteries that must be recharged frequently or they don't work.

iPads: An iPad is a touch screen tablet PC made by Apple. It is basically a tablet without a keyboard. It has a multi-touch LED backlit front display and weighs around 1.5 pounds, with a battery that lasts up to ten hours. The actual size and screen resolution and weight of the iPad depends on the model. Apple now has three different models: the iPad Mini 4, which has a 7.9-inch screen (measured diagonally), the iPad Air with a screen size of

9.7-inch, and the iPad Pro has two versions with screen sizes, 10.5-inch and 12.9-inch.

SMART PHONES

I-Phones: An I-Phone is a smartphone made by Apple combining an iPad, a tablet, a PC, a digital camera and a cellular phone. The device includes Internet browsing and networking capabilities. Batteries also need to be recharged and you must be connected to a network such as Verizon, Sprint, AT&T, and so forth.

There are other operating systems for smart phones, such as Android and Windows.

WHAT DO YOU DO WITH ALL THESE TOYS?

So now that you have an idea of the equipment needed, what do you do with it? Here are more computer terms and a few suggestions.

Software: Software includes programs that run on a computer and perform certain functions.

"Apps": This is a "shorthand" for application. Apps are pieces of hardware that can run on the internet, your phone, tablet, or any electronic device. Apps are typically used to describe anything that isn't a full-fledged software program but a program that is designed to perform a specific function for the user. Users can download both free and purchased apps. Two of the most popular ones are Facebook and Skype.

Facebook: Facebook is a free social networking website that

allows registered users to create profiles, upload photos, send messages and keep in touch with friends. For a tutorial that shows you how to use Facebook, go to: GCFLearnFree or Beginners Guide to Facebook through a Video Tutorial on You Tube, April 22, 2013.

Skype: You can see your family or friend on your computer, if you both have a camera connection. The newer laptops or personal computers have a camera. If you have an older computer, you can add a camera attachment. It's a great way to keep in touch with your grandchildren, especially if you don't yet have an I-phone.

Browser: An internet browser, or web browser, is a software program that you use to access the internet and view web pages on your computer. Think of it as your gateway to the internet. (Examples: Google Chrome, Firefox, Microsoft Internet Explorer, Apple Safari)

I know that this isn't much help, but it is difficult to learn these new technologies without hands on, so take a class...or ask your grandchild how something works. You can always buy (I-Phones) for Dummies. I imagine there are "Dummies" books for all these new "toys".

MORE COMPUTER WORDS THAT MAY CONFUSE

There are so many "new" terms now, many related to computer use. I will try to explain the most common, so you will be knowledgeable about some things. I will try to keep the information as simple as I can, citing basic or essential words. If you want a clearer definition, you will know the word to Google. Now, where to start?

<u>Hardware</u>: the computer, mouse, keyboard, monitor.

<u>Operating System</u>: File management which means creating, saving, naming files and folders, and retrieving them again.

<u>Word-Processing</u>: Open/close/save/save as…documents. Insert text and changing formatting.

<u>Formatting</u>: managing font, size, bold, italics, color, etc.

<u>Font</u>: The combination of typeface and other qualities, such as size, pitch, and spacing.

<u>Processor</u>: The brain of your computer.

<u>RAM</u>: The memory. RAM is what your computer uses to store information while you are using the computer. Also called Random Access Memory.

<u>Operating System</u>: This is the software that makes your computer go. You can buy a computer with the Mac OS X operating system or Windows 10.

<u>Hard Drive</u>: The hard drive is where you will store your files.

<u>URL:</u> URL stands for "Universal Resource Locator". It's another name for a web address.

The above definitions are minimal, just so you will know what to call the device or system, then you can look more information.

I still get confused with these terms. However, lets continue to something I do know about.

TEXTESE

This is what the "texting" language is called; texting is the dearth of correct English. Just ask any English teacher. Textese shortens the words...and destroys proper spelling. Although there are a lot more than I can provide here, I am just letting you know a few, so you can be "cool" when you do text your grandchildren. It is kind of fun. Okay...the list:

LOL...laughing out loud or could be lots of laughs... something that tickles your funny bone.

TGIF...you probably know this one...Thank goodness, it's Friday. I knew this one before computers were popular.

TNX or TY...thank you

BTW...by the way

DIY...do it yourself

HF...have fun

TTYL...talk to you later. My laptop is going crazy. Don't think you have to capitalize all the letters.

IMO...in my opinion. You may not to use this one when you are talking to your children. Remember...they are grown and don't always want your opinion.

NOYB…none of your business. Okay, you can tell your children this…or can you?

YMMD…you made my day. This is a nice one to use.

BRB…be right back.

BFF…best friend forever.

EMOTICONS

Can't leave this chapter without some fun with emoticons. In case you haven't caught on yet, emoticons are a representation of a facial expression such as :-) formed by combination of keyboard characters and used in electronic communications to convey the writer's feelings or intended tone. They have really evolved from their humble beginnings so now when you text, you can tap the smiley face on the bottom of the keyboard and discover hundreds of emoticons. These are the cute little circle faces that show how you are feeling…plus numerous other small items you can add to make a point, like hearts, glasses of wine, animals, flowers, figures, and so much more. Such fun! Lol!

SECURITY STUFF LIKE PINS

You already know about PINs…Personal Identification Numbers. You need a PIN to get money out of the ATM or get into your Fitness Program at the YMCA. You also need a "user name" which is fairly self-explaining. I generally use my email address because it's so "public" and you don't need secrecy here. It's also easy to remember if I use if for everything.

The "pass code" is generally a four-digit number that you need to open your iPhone. A "password" is the "secret word" or expression used by authorized persons to prove their right to access your computer system or electronic device. It is used to open things you don't want others to get into. Just as a secure password is important for security of your online bank account, a secure password is equally necessary to prevent identity theft or scamming of your credit card numbers when you make an online purchase. It should not be your name and birthday or your dog's name. A password should contain both upper and lowercase letters, plus numbers or characters and symbols found on your keyboard, a "code" that is not easy to break. BUT you have to remember it to open your computer also!

Tips: Keep the record of passwords in a safe place and don't forget to update the list when you change your password. Do not carry list in your wallet.

WAYS TO USE THE INTERNET

I have suggested that you "Google" something many times in the above chapters and guess I just assumed that you all know how to Google. (It means do a keyword search on a search engine like Google, not to be confused with Chrome Google which is a browser.) If you don't know, again, just ask a grandchild. There are endless ways that you can "use" the internet; you can look up word spellings or information just like we used to do in a dictionary or set of encyclopedias. Only the search is easier and just takes the fingertips instead of a big book. Computers can be entertaining as well as informative. How many of you are hooked on games, puzzles, solitaire or bridge? Did I say that you can improve your memory by using the internet?

Rich Gray wrote an article about using the internet for Women's Day Magazine back in September, 2000 that listed many of the ways you can "Make money, find out how to fix that leaky faucet, or even just have fun." Here are some of the ideas he presented in his list:

1. Find the weather forecast in your backyard…or anywhere in the world… www.weather.com

2. Help choose a name for the (grand) baby… www.baby-names.com

3. Get the headlines around the world… www.newspaper-links.com

4. Look for a job… www.hotjobs.com or www.monster.com

5. Get coupons to use at the grocery store… www.valpak.com or www.ecoupons.com

6. Look up genealogy or family information… www.ancestry.com

7. How to write to your Congress Member… www.house.gov and www.senate.gov

8. Plan your vacation… www.travelocity.com or www.previewtravel.com

9. Get free craft patterns… www.handcraftervillage.com/freecraft2 or knitting patterns at www.woolworks.org/patterns

10. Play a game at … www.games.yahoo.com

11. Take classes online, for free… www.free-ed.net

12. Play the stock market… www.etrade.com

Guess that will keep your busy enough. If what you are interested in isn't on the list, just Google it. You will probably will find the information you want.

Develop a passion for learning.
If you do, you will never cease to grow.

… Anthony J. D'Angel

10

Apples on a Willow Tree

The significance of this chapters' title? None. It was just something I have remembered from a long time ago. Someone I used to know said that it would be a good title for the book he was going to write...someday. Sorry, Bill, but I beat you to it. (Actually, when I Googled this, the only things I found were Willow Tree Figurines and the best place to grow apples...so don't think he has written that envisioned book yet.) However, this is going to be a fun chapter to write, even if it is not completely relevant for this "self-help guide" I am going to fill it full of the one-liners, stories, poems, and all the interesting items that I have collected throughout the years. I do hope you find something that makes you think, or laugh, or perhaps even cry. I promise to give credit to whomever has written these thoughts...whenever I can find the authors' name. (It is my understanding that one-liners can be used without permission, if I give the author's name. Quotes longer than a few lines must have permission from the author, so I will do my best to comply. Just in case I print something without permission, please forgive me, dear authors. I don't mean to steal your "intellectual property".)

I hope you enjoy reading my whimsical collection. Perhaps a few of the one-liners will make an impression and maybe you will print them on a card and put them on your bathroom mirror so you will remember.

One Liners...I Have No Idea Who Wrote Them

Sign on door... "Out of my mind.... back in five minutes."

Today is the first day of the rest of my life.

Don't worry about tomorrow: God is already there.

Spend your time where you impact the most.

I'll never be "over the hill" ...because I'm too tired to climb up that hill to begin with!

The hardest thing in life is to know which bridge to cross and which to burn.

Lord, give me coffee to change things I can change, and wine to accept the things I can't.

If you have to choose between drinking wine every day or being thin, which would you choose? Red or white?

Instead of calling my bathroom the John, I call my bathroom the Jim. That way it sounds better when I say I go to the Jim first thing every morning.

Don't put a question mark where God put a period.

And God promised men that good and obedient wives would be found in all corners of the world. Then He made the earth round…and laughed and laughed and laughed!

Coincidence is when God chooses to remain anonymous.

Be the person your dog thinks you are.

If God is your co-pilot, change seats.

Best mathematical equation: 1 cross + 3 nails = 4 given.

The way you spend each day adds up to the way you spend your life.

Today's forecast: God reigns and the Son shines.

Love the people God gave you because He will need them back one day.

Life is about leaving and sometimes you don't get to say goodbye.

Forgiveness does not change the past, but it does enlarge the future.

Falling down is part of life; getting back up is living.

Everyone is broken; that's how the light gets in.

A clear conscience is the sign of a fuzzy memory.

You are always responsible for how you act, no matter how you feel.

All God's earth is Holy land.

When my arms can't reach people who are close to my heart, I always hug them with my prayers.

Every time I hear the dirty word "exercise" I wash my mouth out with chocolate! (Thought you would like this one.)

Success: Looking back at your life and the memories make you smile.

MORE ONE LINERS ... WITH AUTHOR CREDIT

"You have not lived today until you have done something for someone who can never repay you." ...John Bunyan

"Show respect even to people who don't deserve it; not as a reflection of their character, but as a reflection of yours." ...Dave Willis

"Nothing happens before first a dream." ...Carl Sandburg

"I have wondered at times what the Ten Commandments would have looked like if Moses had run them through the U.S. Congress." ...Ronald Reagan

"Forgive others not because they deserve forgiveness, but because you deserve peace." ...Johnathan L. Hule

"Most people do not listen with the intent to understand; most people listen with the intent to reply." ...Steven Covey

"Death ends a life, not a relationship" ...Mitch Albam

"I have learned that people will forget what you said, people will forget what you did, but people wil never forget how you made made them feel." ....Maya Angelou

"Be who you are and say what you feel because those who mind don't matter and those who matter don't mind." ...Dr. Seuss

"No one can make you feel inferior without your permission." ...Eleanor Roosevelt

"Whether you think you can, or you can't...either way you're right!" ...Henry Ford

"For every minute you are angry, you lose 60 seconds of happiness." ...Ralph Emerson.

"If you want to know what a man's like, take a look at how he treats his inferiors, not his equals." ... JK Rowling

"In three words, I can sum up everything I've learned about life... it goes on!" ...Robert Frost

"I used to think the worst thing in life is to end up all alone. It's not. The worst thing in life is to end up with people who make you feel all alone." ...Robin Williams

"Age isn't how old you are, but how old you feel." ...Gabriel Garcia Marquez

ADVICE FROM A TREE

- Stand tall and proud
- Go out on a limb
- Remember your roots
- Drink plenty of water
- Be content with your natural beauty
- Enjoy the view

...Ilan Shamir, Face book (10/10/2013)

TEN WAYS TO PLEASE YOURSELF

1. Stop doing things you don't want to do
2. Communicate clearly
3. Stop people pleasing
4. Say what you really mean
5. Trust your instincts
6. Never talk yourself down
7. Follow your inspirations
8. Don't be afraid to say no
9. Don't be afraid to say yes
10. Be kind to yourself.

SCARLETT O'HARA SYNDROME

Do you remember Scarlett from Gone with the Wind? "I'll think about it tomorrow. After all, tomorrow is another day." Daily procrastination! Is that you?

Six Ethics of LIFE

Before you Pray...Believe
Before you Speak...Listen
Before you Spend...Earn
Before you Write...Think
Before you Quit...Try
Before you Die...Live

Other Thoughts and Things to Ponder

"We're taught that there's a prime of life. I say throw that out the door. Every moment is your prime. There is no peak. It just gets better." .... Cindy Joseph, model, (2016)

"Never lose sight of the fact that the most important yardstick of your success will be how you treat other people, your family, friends, and co-workers....and even strangers you meet along the way." ...Barbara Bush

"Focus on the journey, not the destination. Joy is found not in finishing an activity but doing it." ...Greg Anderson

"If you are depressed, you are living in the past. If you are anxious, you are living in the future. If you are at peace, you are living in the present. ...Lao Tzu

Lord, I ask you to protect my children and grandchildren: physically, emotionally, spiritually, mentally, and in every way. Amen.

GENERATIONS

Defined as "all the people born and living at about the same time." It can also be described as, "the average period generally considered to be about thirty years, during which children are born and grow up, become adults, and begin to have children" …according to Wikipedia. The title Baby Boomers was the only one "defined" by the US Census Bureau after WWII ended. The rest were named by the news media. Here are the birth years for each generation:

- Depression Baby: Born 1926-1935
- War Baby: Born 1936-1945
- (Traditionalists or Silent Generation: Born 1945 and before)
- Baby Boomers: Born 1946 to 1964
- Generation X: Born 1965-1976
- Millennials or Gen Y: Born 1977-1995
- Gen Z, iGen, or Centennials: Born 1996 and later

So, which generation are you? I'm not sure that the "Silent Generation" is a correct title for me! I am a War Baby, however, born just months before Pearl Harbor bombing.

A VETERAN

A veteran, whether active duty, discharged, retired or reserve, is someone who, at one point in his/her life wrote a blank check made payable to "The United States of America", for an amount of "up to and including his/her life." It is an honor to be a veteran. There are too many people in this country today who no longer understand that fact!

"Patriotism is easy to understand in America; it means looking out for yourself by looking out for your country." …Calvin Coolidge

WHAT PERCENTAGE OF AMERICANS HAVE SERVED IN THE MILITARY?

As of 2014, the VA estimates there were 22 million military veterans in the U.S. population. If you add the active military personnel number of our population (1.4 million), that means 7.3% of all living Americans have served in the military at some point in their lives. This seems to be the latest figures. You must discount all the veterans who have died in the past three years. Many of these dear veterans have been interviewed by volunteers and their stories are recorded for posterity at the Library of Congress in the Veterans History Project. They are always looking for volunteers to conduct these interviews. If you are interested, contact www. loc/vhp.gov . I have been interviewing these wonderful veterans for years and each one has as story to tell. Each one is a humble hero!

More facts: The Pentagon states that 71% of today's youth between 17 and 24 would be ineligible for military service because of medical, academic, and moral standards. Many cannot pass the physical to join the military! To pass the physical one must be able to meet three challenges: two minutes of push-ups, two minutes of sit-ups, and complete a two-mile run in 15 minutes and 54 seconds or less! Grandparents…should we talk to our grandchildren about "getting physical"?

My husband was a West Point graduate, Class of 1962, who served in the Army for over 20 years. He was patriotic and physically fit!

COINS ON GRAVE MARKERS

Have you ever noticed that some grave markers have coins on top of them? This is what they mean to the military: a penny means you visited the grave. A nickel means you trained at Bootcamp together. A dime means your served together. A quarter means you were there when the soldier was killed.

At Arlington National Cemetery the money is collected after Memorial Day and used for cemetery maintenance, burial costs and care for indigent soldiers.

A WIDOW'S THOUGHTS

Sometimes being a widow means: Sitting in front of a campfire in October, with a glass of wine. The fire is perfect to take off the chill of the autumn night and keep the mosquitoes away. It is just after sunset on a beautiful fall day. The hot dogs are ready to roast in the glowing coals. I am alone...just me and my dog.

I am missing you...but remembering the lovely evenings we shared beside a similar fire, on a similar Fall evening. You might be gone...but your memory lingers on...and on!

...I wrote this when I was here at Wilderness in October, 2012. At the time, I had been a widow for five years.

Those we love don't go away,
They walk beside us every day.
Unseen, unheard, but always near,
Still loved, still missed and very dear. .... Matt Fraser

Greet each day as if it were brand new…it is! Let go of what happened yesterday and focus on the sweetness of a new beginning unfolding before you.

ASAP=Always Say a Prayer

STOP= Savor the Observable Presence of God

BIBLE= Basic Instructions Before Leaving Earth

There are lots of choices to make in life; in eternity, there are only two.

GRANDMOTHERS

A word from all grandmothers… As I grew older, I thought the best part of my life was over. Then I was handed my first grandchild and realized the best part of my life had just begun!

Excerpts from <u>Angel in Marble</u>, by Elaine Coffman

"My old body is just wearing out. I've been dreaming of your grandpa a lot lately. It's the same dream over and over. I see him looking so young! Like he did when I married him. It's like he's waiting for me and I think he probably is. He's been gone so many years now, but I still love him as strongly as I ever did. I suppose that's why I could never remarry.

I've had a good, long life with more blessings than I can count. But I've been away from your grandpa too long, and I think it's time I went home. The obstinate beating of this old heart of mine is beginning to sound more and more like a funeral bell. I gave my granddaughter my silver watch. It's a reminder that time doesn't stand still for us, no matter how much we dawdle along the way. Time passes, but it leaves its shadow. God sends us opportunity, but He won't wake us if we're asleep."

WHEN I SAY, "I AM A CHRISTIAN"

When I say, "I am a Christian" I am not shouting "I've been saved!"
I am whispering, "I get lost sometimes That's why I chose this way."

When I say, "I am a Christian" I don't speak with humble pride
I'm confessing that I stumble Needing God to be my guide.

When I say, "I am a Christian" I'm not trying to be strong
I'm professing that I am weak And pray for strength to carry on.

When I say, "I am a Christian" I'm not bragging of success
I'm admitting that I have failed And cannot ever pay the debt.

When I say, "I am a Christian" I don't think I know it all
I submit to my confusion Asking humbly to be taught.

When I say, "I am a Christian" I'm not claiming to be perfect
My flaws are all too visible But God believes I'm worth it.

When I say, "I am a Christian" I still feel the sting of pain
I have my share of heartache That's why I see God's name.

When I say, "I am a Christian" I do not wish to judge
I have no authority I only know I'm loved.

...This lovely poem was written in 1988 by Carol Wimmer. An altered version of the poem has been misattributed to Dr. Maya Angelou. (This poem was used by permission. Carol Wimmer, www.carolwimmer.com)

SENIOR KNOWLEDGE

Some people embrace their golden years, while others become bitter and surly. Life is too short to waste your days on the latter.

Spend your time with positive, cheerful people, it'll rub off on you and your days will seem that much better. Spending your time with bitter people will make you older and harder to be around.

Never use the phrase "In my time." Your time is now. As long as you're alive, you are part of this time. You may have been younger, but you are still now, having fun and enjoying life.

CAMP RULES

Wake up smiling. Be grateful.
Read a book...relax and unwind.
Watch the Sunset.
LOVE. Go for a nature walk, play with the grands.
Enjoy one another.
Toast marshmallows...wish on the stars.
Catch a fish

Eat too much…Take a nap, take a photo, take a breath.
Make memories. LAUGH.
Count your blessings.

…This was copied from a sign, composed by my friend Clara from across the lake. It epitomizes the activities at this place called Wilderness. I thought it was also great "general rules" for anyone.

THE BONFIRES OF LIFE

Have you ever thought of your life as similar to a bonfire?

One must prepare for a bonfire…or for a new life.

It takes time for a flame to be ignited…and 9 months for life to begin.

At first, it's a flicker…needs help…and more help…as united cells develop and grow.

A small flame has caught…will the embryo survive?

The wood must be positioned to catch the flame…or it goes out.

Okay, we have a small flame…and a new life. A baby is born! YEA!

But it requires constant care, lest it burns out before it can burn alone.

Ok? It's caught! A beautiful fire… And the child grows. Lots of work to raise a child. All those diapers and baby foods!

And…both the fire and child will need nurturing…more wood, more air…a little extra help perhaps…okay, it's well established at last. Infancy, toddler, youth…all that education…love, support and nurturing … to graduation.

One can sit back and enjoy…the light, the heat…the career…the adult life.

For a while…but wait…the flames are gone! No, it just needs more wood, more help. Life is like that…there are peaks and valleys.

Just more adjustment of the wood and there you are…a brilliant fire once more…and a successful life.

Enjoy it now…learn from it…watch it glow.

Again…and then again…the flame falters…but help is there to convince it to continue with heat and light…aging does that also.

Occasionally a flame shoots up, but now there's just a red glow in the ashes…but wait, there's another flame… It's gone again.

This may take longer with some fires than others…just as some lives are longer than others.

Some may be dashed with unwelcomed high winds or rain… the end before the end…only to blaze up once again…or go out. Likewise, there are diseases or accidents that occur, causing a premature death.

I hope my flame is constant until all the wood is consumed…and that there is a lesson in the ashes!!!

I have lived…and flamed up…died down and re-flamed again… with smoke that makes everything unclear…but I held on to my ashes …to flame again…and again.

Yes, life is like a bonfire. Some are better built…and longer lasting than others.

May your life be as long as a well built, long-lasting bonfire.

…Pati Redmond

PLACES

The nicest place to be is in someone's thoughts,

The safest place to be is in someone's prayers.

The best place to be is in the hands of God.

THINGS THAT MAY DISAPPEAR IN OUR LIFETIME

- the Book
- the Check
- the Post Office
- the Newspaper
- the Landline phone
- Woodburning fireplaces
- Privacy
- Glasses
- Cameras
- House keys
- Plastic bags
- Cursive writing

FOREVER IN MY HEART

You can shed a tear that he is gone, or you can smile because he lived.

You can close your eyes and pray that he'll come back or you can open your eyes and see all he's left.

You can be empty because you can't see him, or you can be full of the love you shared.

You can turn your back on today and live in yesterday or you can be happy for tomorrow because of yesterday.

You can remember only that he is gone, or you can cherish the memory and let it live on.

You can cry and close your mind, be empty and turn your back, or you can do what he'd want...smile, open your eyes, love and let go.

You can remember only that he has gone, or you can cherish his memory and let it live on.

...No author listed, Facebook (March 11, 2016)

"Just one small positive thought in the morning, can change your whole day."

...Dalai Lama

11

Memories are Better than Dreams

My esteemed husband, who taught at the United States Military Academy at West Point for three years, told me, "When you give a lecture or a talk always tell the audience what you are going to say, say it, and then tell them again what you have said!" I do hope this is the same technique to use when you are writing a "self-help guide." If so, this is the last step in my book. I will just tell you again what I have told you in the last ten chapters. I know, some people always turn to the last chapter to see how the book ends before reading it. If you are that person, look at the time you have saved.

WE THE WIDOWS... IN REVIEW

Just looked up "review" and one of the definitions is a general examination or criticism of a recent work." Okay, that sounds about right. Hope there's not too much criticism. Here is your review.

- This book was written for you...the widow.
- Death of a spouse happens...to women more often to men.
- Immediate decisions after death...funeral arrangements and all the required actions

- Practical matters you will take care of
- You can survive your grief. You are still "vertical and ventilating".
- Help in getting over grief…and decreasing stress in your life
- Endings are also beginnings. This is a new beginning to the rest of your life.
- Find your own "peaceful" place, where you can go to relax, think, remember and make plans…or just to watch the flowers grow.
- Find a passion in life…something you love to do.
- Don't rely on your children to "take the place of your husband."
- Know that you will make mistakes…forgive yourself and learn from them.
- Be brave: acknowledge changes you need to make.
- Be positive in thoughts, actions, and attitude.
- Laugh at yourself.
- Keep up with the current events in our world.
- Remember the good times…but make more memories, especially if you are blessed with grandchildren.
- The anticipation of anniversaries is worse than the actual day.
- Don't whine or complain about things like your health, situation, or loneliness.
- Pray.
- Age gracefully…you are no longer a teenager, but you don't care!
- Birthdays are good; congrats! You've lived another year.
- Taking care of YOU…health, diet, appearance and other cares
- Possible health challenges
- Did I talk about exercising too much?

- Safety matters…especially in your home and in your car.
- Financial matters…will your income be enough?
- Watch out for frauds and scams; seniors are fair game to bad people.
- Enjoy your money; you have earned it! And you don't have to save it for your children.
- A shredder is a good purchase.
- Your home still needs to be cleaned.
- Take care of your appliances.
- Take care of your auto, lawn mower and other mechanical stuff.
- Tips and more tips. Too many?
- It's a couples' world…but make it yours, too.
- Friendships are golden. Some are there for a short term… others forever. Enjoy each and every friend.
- Computers and electronics are amazing, if somewhat confusing…and can be quite useful to seniors.
- Apples don't grow on willow trees, but ideas and sayings do and may give you something to think about.
- Trees give good advice.
- We are a sisterhood of widows.

How's that for a synopsis? Hope I didn't forget anything useful.

SOME MORE POSITIVE THINGS MY WIDOWED FRIENDS SAID

"You will change. If your husband could see the person you've become, he might say who made off with my wife? The status quo is gone; reinvent yourself."

"The worst has happened. Be ready for a new beginning."

"God is good and will walk with us as we enter this new phase of our lives."

"You must love yourself before you can love anyone else."

"Life is about leaving and sometimes you don't get to say goodbye."

"Accept that every stage in life brings something beautiful; that's how you enjoy life."

"It is comforting to think that my children don't feel I am depending on them for happiness in life. I love letting them know that I am involved in many things on my own. It gives them happiness to know that I am an independent soul now. It gives me happiness to know that they are there for me in any way I need them."

Another widow's comments: "Widow: I hated that word! In the beginning after John's death, I didn't think I could survive alone… could take care of things. But day by day passed and I did! I found that I could do everything John did with the help of my family and friends. I was not alone. I just took one day at a time."

And I would tell my dear departed husband, "Your West Point Class of 1962 motto, "62 Can Do!" has worked for me! I have learned to do a lot of things that I never thought I could."

PROMISE FULFILLED

I did promise you in Chapter One that I'd tell you why I never worked a day in my life as a Physical Therapist. Just in case you are still interested, I will explain now. When I was a sophomore at

Ohio State University, the trees on the Oval were still twigs, and I thought I wanted to have a career as a medical technologist. Then I took college chemistry…and hated it! I didn't want to be dealing with test tubes all my life. Therefore, it followed that I would not like medical technology as a career.

Two of my new friends, who were also in that chemistry class, told me that they were headed for a career in Physical Therapy and thought I would be good in that field. This is when the idea was born. I didn't really know what Physical Therapy was…it was a relatively new profession, and I hadn't heard much about it. I looked into it and it seemed to be "made for me."! I was accepted into the Physical Therapy Program my junior year and I loved it from the beginning of the training. At that time, a PT degree required only graduating with a four-year Bachelor of Science degree, three one-month clinical affiliations for "on the job training" and then acquiring a license to practice in the state where you would work.

I graduated and started working as a physical therapist, a career that lasted for over forty years. I loved it so much and enjoyed helping all my patients achieve their goals. It never felt like work! This could be a nugget of wisdom you could pass on to your grandchildren. It doesn't matter what you do, but you should love your job. It sure makes life so much more pleasant!

And I am pleased to say that I passed on that wisdom to my daughter Erin, who has her Doctorate of Physical Therapy. She, too, loves her job…although the requirements for physical therapy have changed to seven years of college!

When I returned to Ohio State University for a football game a few years ago I noticed that the trees on the Oval have grown to make a gigantic canopy for students to walk through. They have aged well, too.

PONDERING

I am wondering how long this book will be useful before it becomes obsolete. Things evolve so quickly. My husband's grandmother was born in the "horse and buggy" age, had a long eventful life and died at the age of 102, after our astronauts had landed on the moon! Just imagine what she experienced in her lifetime!

However, things are changing faster than they ever did in the "horse and buggy" age. But I am comforted in thinking that this book can be an example for future generations to learn about life in the 21st century…and it may teach them a thing or two.

DREAMS AND MEMORIES

So, have you deduced that memories are better than dreams? Perhaps dreams are just memories that haven't happened yet. Although I never dreamed of being a widow, the memories of the past ten years are sweet. I have endeavored to become the best person I can be…and I am still in the process, striving to achieve this goal. Dreams and goals move you forward and help you create your life. Don't forget to enjoy the little things along the way that make life so wonderful. You will find many moments to savor…and then they will become memories.

I know now that the grief caused by your husband's death never ends, but it changes. It's a passage, not a place to stay. Grief isn't a sign of weakness, nor a lack of faith… it is the price of love.

SISTERHOOD OF WIDOWS

Death shakes our self-awareness of who we are.
If you're not a Mrs. Anymore, who are you?
Before re-entry into single living, you must redefine yourself.

First step is to learn to be a single person, ready and able to face life alone.
Second step is learning to love again which includes learning to love yourself.
Then you learn to accept yourself as you are.
That gives you permission to grow, change and become the person you want to be.

We all have had traumatic experience that have left us wounded.
But these events are part of life and part of living.
Your life is in your control, so feel love for yourself.
It is the way life is meant to be.

I have enjoyed every minute writing this book for you. Nevertheless...

…. All good things must come to: The End.

…And the End Date, just like summer: Labor Day, September 4, 2017.

However, "The End" only applies to this book. There is a new beginning for you and perhaps this book has given you some tools to work with. Reread the chapters that helped you the most, and don't forget to laugh at my silliness this time. My blessings and prayers go with you as you move forward into your new life.

We must be willing to let go of the life we have planned, so as to have the life that is waiting for us.

...E.M. Forster

Acknowledgement

I would first like to thank each and every widow who contributed their thoughts, ideas and comments to this book. I will list their names in no particular order. I do appreciate and want to thank: Anna Brown, Elinor Currie, Vesta Pearigen, Mary Ruth Geise, Nery Quintela, Margaret Scott, Jan Sturdevent, Fanny Johnson, Mary Stansfield, Linda Nelson, Suzi Parero, Gale Loberg, Ida Lu Brown, Coralinn Kuehl, Ann Martin, Kathleen Constable, Florence Schell, Donna Cuseo, Mikki Carpenter, Kathleen Eames, Marty-Mercer-Akre, Nella Hunter, Pat Warner, Virginia Sumner, Carolyn Peal, Clair Williams, Kathleen Eames, and Judy King.

Also sending gratitude to my "tech support" Mike and Darla Brown who rescued my book from computer "madness" while at Wilderness and Seline Mejia who helped me out of computer messes when at home, to my "editor" Paula Nossett, and friends Jane and Carlos Mercado for their helpful comments. Thanks also to John Buchiemer. I could never have mowed my yard for ten years without his help, and to his wife Pat who doesn't mind when I talk to John.

·ACKNOWLEDGEMENT

I'd also like to thank Jack Brubaker for advising me on which laptop to purchase, to my friend Jane Mercado for her ideas and for being the first person who told me she liked this book, and Anna Brown, the first widow to read it. And last, but not least, thanks to my wonderful daughters Erin Webb and Jackie Overton for their support and encouragement. I am truly blessed by these two wonderful daughters, their husbands and ten awesome grandchildren.

Appendices

Navy Mutual Survivor Checklist

This checklist has been prepared to help survivors address a variety of concerns involved in caring for the affairs of a deceased person. It is not all inclusive and is not intended to replace legal counsel where services of an attorney may be desirable or necessary.

Casuality Assistance Calls Officer

Survivors of a military member who dies on active duty will be assigned a Causality Assist Calls Officer (CACO) to be their liaison with the service. The CACO is there to help survivors coordinate funeral arrangements and apply for benefits and entitlements. The CACO is not a subject matter expert, but is trained to answer general questions and to refer survivors to the appropriate expert or agency to assist them.

OBTAIN

❑ Several original copies of the death certificate (funeral director will usually provide)

REVIEW

❏ Survivor's life insurance policy(ies) as well as other policies; revise as appropriate

NOTIFY

Insurance companies: ❏ Life ❏ Auto ❏ Health
❏ Internal Revenue Service (IRS) for potential forgiveness of decedent's tax liability
❏ Department of Motor Vehicles (DMV)
❏ Social, fraternal, academic, or religious organizations

Accounts held by the deceased:
❏ Financial
❏ Investment/TSP/401(k)
❏ Credit/Recurring Payments CACO FOR LIFE

UPDATE

❏ Survivor's Will, Power of Attorney, Durable Power of Attorney, and/or Living Will as necessary

RENEW

❏ Military identification card

CONTACT

❏ All Veterans Service Organizations (VSO) of which the deceased was a member
❏ Defense Enrollment Eligibility Reporting System (DEERS)

- ❏ Defense Finance and Accounting Services (DFAS)
- ❏ Department of Veterans Affairs (VA)
- ❏ Employer of the deceased
- ❏ The Social Security Administration (SSA)
- ❏ US Coast Guard (USCG)(PPC)

Upon separation or retirement, a veteran's survivors are no longer provided a CACO to assist in navigating government benefits. Navy Mutual provides "CACO for Life" services to all Navy Mutual members and their survivors. Navy Mutual personnel will assist members and their survivors with obtaining VA benefits--disability compensation; pensions; special monthly compensation (often known as aid and attendance); burial benefits; survivor benefits; which include dependency and indemnity compensation (DIC); and survivors' and dependents' educational assistance (DEA).

Additionally, Navy Mutual's VA-accredited Veteran Service Representatives assist veterans and their dependents with the preparation, presentation, and prosecution of initial claims to the Veterans Benefits Administration (VBA) or appeals to the Board of Veterans' Appeals (BVA).

Contact a Navy Mutual Veteran Service Representative for more details. vso@navymutual.org or 1-800-628-6011

Navy Mutual Planning Checklist

Making sure your family is knowledgeable about a variety of personal financial and family issues is important. Experts recommend preparing some type of a personal log to document this information. There are a number of steps that can be taken in advance to help transition go smoother for family members grieving the loss of a loved one.

Inital Steps

- ❏ Does each spouse/beneficiary have a general understanding of the family's assets and investments? This includes knowing where the money is and why it is there.
- ❏ Does each spouse/beneficiary know where all important documents are: financial statements, insurance policies, deeds, wills and trust?
- ❏ Does each spouse/beneficiary have website login information and know who to contact when needed?
- ❏ Does each spouse/beneficiary have a will, an advance medical directive and a durable power of attorney? Military Legal Assistance can assist active duty, retirees, and their families with this. Does each spouse know the others wishes regarding life support and quality of life issues?
- ❏ Does each spouse/beneficiary know where records of previous and current year IRS materials are kept?
- ❏ Are medical and dental records up to date? Does each spouse/beneficiary know where those records are kept or how to access them?

Important Documents

Keep one hard copy or digital folder with original/copies of important documents in a safe storage location, preferably outside the home. Keep another folder with copies of these documents in an easily accessible and secure location.

- ❏ Marriage, Birth, and Death Certificates
- ❏ Wills and Trust
- ❏ Financial Records and Insurance Beneficiaries
- ❏ Advance Medical Directives and Powers of Attorney
- ❏ Summary of VA Benefits
- ❏ DD Form 214
- ❏ Social Security Administration Summary of Benefits
- ❏ Divorce Decrees
- ❏ Adoption Papers
- ❏ Naturalization Papers
- ❏ Vehicle Title and Registration Papers
- ❏ Leave and Earnings Statement (LES) or Retiree Account Statement (RAS)
- ❏ Medical Treatment Records

References

Coffman, Elaine. (1991) <u>Angel in Marble.</u> New York, NY. Ballantine Publishing Group.

Fleet, Carol Brody. (2009) <u>Widows Wear Stilettos, A Practical and Emotional Guide for the Young Widow.</u> Far Hill, NJ. New Horizon Press.

Kubler-Ross, Elizabeth & David Kessler. (2005) <u>On Grief and Grieving</u>. New York, NY. Simon & Schuster.

Marshall, Ann Hall. (2010). <u>Crooked Lines</u>. Seattle, WA: 1564 Publishing.

Marshall, Ann Hall. (2012). <u>Full Measure of Love</u>. Seattle, WA: 1564. Publishing.

Marshall, Ann Hall. (2014). <u>Dori's Life</u>. South Carolina: Create Space

MOAA Info Exchange. <u>Turning the Corner; Surviving the Loss of a Loved One</u>. "Signs You're Getting Better". Alexandria, VA. p. 18-19

McKenna, Paul. (2012). <u>I Can make You Smarter</u>. London. Transworld Publishers.

Quinn, Jane Bryant. (2009). <u>Making the Most of Your Money Now</u>. New York, NY. Simon and Schuster

Shoemaker, Jane Woods. (2003). <u>Widows Walk</u>. San Luis Obispo, CA. Lodestar Publications.

A Note from the Author

I hope you have enjoyed reading <u>We the Widows...A Guide to Your New Life</u>.

If you would like a copy, perhaps to give to another widow, or even keep for yourself, I can be reached at:

Pati Redmond   or   WetheWidows@gmail.com
7503 Ridge Road
Frederick, MD, 21702

We the Widows can also be purchased online from Amazon.com, or at Barnes and Noble. It can also be ordered at your favorite book store.

I would love to hear your comments, questions or even more advice for widows. It will be too late for this edition, but who knows, maybe I will do a revised version later and include your suggestions.

CPSIA information can be obtained
at www.ICGtesting.com
Printed in the USA
BVHW06s2257081018
529576BV00005B/152/P